# The M᷄  ᴜnd

## (How I almost made it in the Music Industry)

Martin Davies

The Million Pound Drop.
Copyright © Martin Davies 2017

All rights reserved.

ISBN: 978-1973873877

For Jayne x

# Introduction/foreword

I started writing this book in February 2015. At that time, I had reached a crossroads in my life and felt quite lost.

Initially, the book was going to be a snapshot of my life whilst working in the music industry. However, as I started writing, I found myself re-counting musical anecdotes from my youth, and so decided to cast the net a little wider.

I was also conscious of the fact that there may come a point in the future, where it would feel like the experiences had never even happened, lost forever in the dark recesses of my mind.

So here it is, as I remember it.

Martin Davies, Wolverhampton February 2017.

*Some days will stay a thousand years*
*Some pass like the flash of a spark*
*Who knows where all our days go...*
Stuart Adamson, 1984

# *Act 1*

# *Chapters:*

Prologue....................*The fall*                                  1

*Vinyl addiction and
obsessive compulsive disorder*                                7

*Under the stars, petrol bombs and
borrowing cars*                                                       27

*Pat-a-cake, pat-a-cake, baker's man*               38

*Are Friends Electric?*                                            47

*Speed freaks and self-harm*                                  61

*University of Wolverhampton and
cock-blocking Simon Le Bon*                               74

*An Actor's Life for Me*                                         86

*Put the Needle Down and Fly*                             96

*Hang the DJ*                                                        105

## Prologue
## The fall

Wednesday 25th November 1991 was like any other working day. The only difference between this particular day and the two previous days was that there had been a significant drop in temperature. The prevailing wind was icy cold and there was a ground frost, which made my normal walk more like a shuffle, for fear of slipping over.

I was an employee of J.B. Makin Roofing Contractors Ltd, which was based in Wednesbury in the West Midlands. I was twenty years old and had been working for the company for two years.

I had been sent to Stoke-On-Trent, to complete a roof repair on a new house. It was a routine job, which would usually take around twenty minutes to complete.

It wasn't until I actually arrived at the building site, that I realized just how bad the weather conditions were. The usual soft dirt underfoot was now solid. This often creates problems when trying to use a ladder, because you can't wedge the base of it into the ground, so there is a danger that the ladder will slide, unless of course, you have a work mate to foot the ladder whilst you climb it or scaffolding with which you can tie the ladder to, neither of which I had.

To make matters even worse, I hadn't brought a cat-ladder with me. This is like a normal ladder, but has a hook on the end, so you can attach it to the top of a house roof, thus allowing you to climb the roof safely.

I was going to have to improvise. Now, when tiling a roof you only put nails in every fourth row

1

of tiles, this means that the tiles which aren't nailed can often be pushed up by about four inches, creating steps. But on this particular day, try as I might, I just couldn't push any tiles up, because they were fused together by the frost.

I had to make a decision; leave the repair job, which wouldn't go down well with my boss, or take a risk and attempt to walk up the roof.

Now I have to point out that health and safety was never high on the agenda with employees of J.B. Makin. The main reason for this is that workers often like to cut corners to make the job easier. Put purely and simply, it's just laziness. For example, I once had to complete four repairs on a building site in Walsall. The repairs were on four different houses, which were situated all in a row. Now instead of putting the ladder up onto each individual house, I just decided to jump across each house roof to complete the repairs.

To be fair, the gap between each house roof was only about three feet wide. However, it's still not a sensible thing to do. I did it to save time and to get out of the hassle of keep moving and climbing the ladder. There you go ... laziness.

I had jumped across to the third house when I heard a very loud voice cry out, "Hey! Get off that fucking roof." I looked towards the ground, completely oblivious to the fact that the angry voice was actually being directed at me. Again it cried out, "Yes, I am talking to you roofer, get off my fucking roof!" I flew back across the roofs and descended my ladder, only to come face to face with the site foreman. He was furious.

"Get your tools together and get your arse off my site."

"I am really sorry. It was stupid I won't do it again," I replied.

"I couldn't give a shit, get your tools and get off the site."

So off I popped, in a panic, thinking my boss would go crazy. Then unbelievably, as I was driving off the site, my boss was arriving onto the site. I couldn't believe his bloody timing.

My boss stopped the car and wound his window down, "Have you done those repairs already?" he asked.

"No, the foreman has kicked me off the site. I am sorry Steve. He caught me jumping the roofs."

Surprisingly, my boss didn't even raise his voice.

"Right, go back to the yard and wait for me."

So I drove back to the yard, where our work's offices and supplies were situated and awaited the arrival of my boss.

About forty five minutes later, my boss turned up.

"I have smoothed things over with the foreman. You can go back and finish those jobs now."

The irony of this entire situation, was that six weeks earlier, I had won a Toby meal for two after coming first place in the work's health and safety worker of the month competition.

Anyway, I digress. Back to November 25th, I was about to make another stupid decision, one which certainly wouldn't result in any kind of health and safety award. I decided to walk up the roof.

I slowly eased myself off the ladder and onto the house roof (which was approximately 25ft high) and slowly made my way up the tiles, claw-hammer in one hand and plastic replacement ridge cap in the other.

I was really taking my time, as there were still patches of heavy frost on the roof. One foot in front of the other I was gradually getting closer to the pinnacle of the roof, when suddenly, I slipped. The first pain I felt was the impact of my back hitting the tiles, it forced the wind out of my lungs and I struggled to get my breath.

I started to slide down the roof and quickly let go of my hammer, so I could use my hands to try and stop myself. It was no good, try as I might, I just couldn't get any grip on the tiles. Not only that, but I was also really building up quite a momentum. The only thing that could save me now was the ladder. I was hoping and praying that this would stop my fall ... but when my feet hit the ladder, it just kicked the ladder away from the roof and I slipped straight over the edge.

You often hear people screaming in movies, when they fall off a cliff or a tall building. I can now confirm that this is completely involuntary. As I slid off the roof, I screamed "Aaaaahhhhh!!!" Then in what seemed like a split second, I landed with a thud, feet first on the ground below.

I was terrified to move at first, thinking I must have done serious damage to myself. I tried moving my toes, they seemed ok, I then felt my legs and they seemed ok too. I just lay there in shock. Suddenly a plumber appeared beside me. He had been working inside the house and heard my scream. He told me not to move and said he'd go and get some help. About a minute later, I started to feel an intense pain in my right foot. A sense of panic hit me like a tidal wave. It was no good I had to take my boot off, to see the damage. I slowly undid my laces and eased my boot off, then peeled my sock down to reveal my foot. It was black. I just lay back on the ground and waited for help.

It didn't take long to arrive, four site workers

appeared and carried me into the back of a van and I was whisked off to the local hospital.

My neck, back and legs were all checked and amazingly they were fine. The doctors couldn't believe it. I had fallen off a two-storey building and my back and legs were completely intact. My foot was now the major concern but all the x ray revealed was one fractured metatarsal.

"You are one lucky man," the doctor said.

"Is that it?" I asked. "Am I ok?"

"Yes, we'll just get your foot in plaster and then you can go home."

"What about work?" I asked.

"Oh, you won't be back on another roof for at least eleven weeks."

I had reached a point after two years, where I'd really begun to hate my job, so this was sweet music to my ears. I was about to put my feet up for eleven weeks. It's amazing how quickly the shock of the accident began to dissipate.

My brother collected me from the hospital and just by chance, as we were approaching Stafford on the M6 motorway, I saw two of my work colleagues in the near side lane, travelling back from a job.

I said to my brother, "Pap the horn... Quick!"

"What do you mean?"

"Pap the bloody horn, I want to wave at the guys."

As my brother overtook the J.B. Makin van, hooting the horn, I wound down the window, stuck my head out and shouted, "Woo hoo, eleven weeks off work, read it and weep!"

My leg was resting on the dashboard, in a huge white plaster and I had a grin on my face from ear to ear.

I think there is a big part of me that has always

believed in fate. Someone was watching over me that day. The accident could have, and I suppose a lot people would say, SHOULD have been horrific. But it wasn't. What it did do however, although I didn't know it at the time, was send my life in a completely different and dramatic direction.

## *Vinyl addiction and obsessive compulsive disorder*

The first records I ever bought were 'Party Fears Two' by The Associates and 'Glittering Prize' by Simple Minds, both were on 7 inch single. It was 1982 and I was 12 years old. Up to this point, my only experience of music had been listening to my uncle's Led Zeppelin collection at my gran's house, circa 1978 and then later, sitting in my bedroom listening to what my brother was playing on his stereo. My brother was a New Romantic, a pop culture movement that had started in London nightclubs such as The Blitz in the late 70s and early 80s. You could often identify a New Romantic, by their flamboyant clothes and face make-up, which was worn by both women and men. The bands most closely linked to this movement, were the likes of Duran Duran, Spandau Ballet and Visage.

My brother, Ian, had a fantastic collection of records, which consisted of a real diverse mix of artists, not just New Romantic bands, but artists such as David Bowie, The Jam, Talk Talk, Japan and punk bands like The Sex Pistols, The Plasmatics and The Exploited. He even collected records by the more obscure New Romantic bands, like The Mood, who were a one-hit-wonder with their single 'Paris is One Day Away'. Actually, upon further research, I discovered that this wasn't a hit at all, as it didn't even enter the top 40. So who knows how my brother discovered this one.

Sometimes, I used to sit on my brother's bed and watch him getting ready to go out on a Friday or Saturday night. He'd be blasting out Duran

Duran's debut album, whilst donning his frilly shirt, pleated trousers and pixie boots. I always thought he looked quite glamorous, but at the same time a little effeminate, certainly not your stereotypical idea of a working-class teenager. But then, I think that was the whole point.

When Ian wasn't in, I used to camp out in his room and flick through all of his vinyl. I started to become obsessed with the record sleeves. For me the covers were almost as important as the music. I remember the cartoon cover of XTC's 'Sgt Rock', which featured a goofy looking soldier marching across a battlefield and The Jam's minimalist cover for their single 'Start!' which was plain pink, with the words The Jam and Start! In bold black letters. They were very different covers but equally fascinating.

Another cover that stood out to me, but for all the wrong reasons, featured a cartoon dog, dressed as Superman. It turned out to be a song called 'Ruff Mix' by Wonder Dog. The song was awful and featured samples of dogs barking. I mean, who wants to listen to dogs barking? Well my brother, obviously.

The song was recorded by German artist Harry Thumann, but a man named Simon Cowell obtained the rights to it and promoted it in the UK. Apparently, it peaked at number 32 in the UK singles chart. Yes, this was indeed evidence that my brother would buy anything.

I used to make mix tapes on my brother's stereo, so I could play them on my Sony Walkman.C60 cassette tapes were the best, they allowed for 30 minutes of audio per side. I always found that C90 and C120 tapes were less reliable (my Walkman used to chew them up) you would then have to try and rescue the recording, by untangling the tape from the capstan, then winding it back into your cassette using a pencil.

One of my favourite home-made mix tapes included the following songs:

The Lotus Eaters – 'The First Picture of You'
H2O – 'Dream to Sleep'
China Crisis – 'Wishful Thinking'
Freur – 'Doot Doot
OMD – 'Souvenir'

After dipping my toes into the New Romantic genre, I pretty much started to embrace all kinds of music. A friend named Wayne Stokes introduced me to the American band Kiss, who I thought were cool for a while, because just like the New Romantics, they also wore make up. However, they were rock, so the music was heavier.

I also went through a Mod phase, where I was listening to bands like The Who and Small Faces. There was a Mod clothing store in Walsall called Smart Guys and I used to pester my mum to buy me badger shoes, Union Jack t shirts and jumpers. Badger shoes were black suede shoes with white stripes down the front and sides. They were also known as 'Jam' shoes, because The Jam's bass player, Bruce Foxton could be seen wearing them in the video for The Jam's number one single 'Going Underground'.

My dad would make sarcastic comments, like, "You want badger shoes. Shoes made from badgers!"

"No, they are called badger shoes, because they are black and white."

I remember buying a white t shirt with a huge target on the front, another Mod classic.

My dad piped up, "Well you are just asking for

it now."

"Asking for what?"

"You are asking for someone to take a shot."

"What do you mean?"

"Wearing a huge target like that."

"Oh yes very funny. It had completely slipped my mind that Moxley was the gun capital of the UK."

That said, to be fair, you did often see some of the Moxley youth messing around with air rifles. I had messed around with them myself. Perhaps my dad had a point.

From the Mod movement, to hip hop! Yes, I even got into break dancing. The Street Sounds Electro compilation tapes had started to become popular in the UK around 1984, along with a film called *Beat Street*. This was a movie about two brothers who were involved in the hip hop scene. The younger brother is a break dancer and the older one a DJ. The film was set in the Bronx, New York.

The film features an iconic break dance competition at the Roxy nightclub, featuring the New York City Breakers vs The Rock Steady Crew. I must have watched this scene about fifty times. I would try to remember the moves, and recreate them on a piece of cardboard on my front lawn. The scene is up on Youtube I believe. You should check it out, it's old school breakdancing at its very best.

My mates were all music fanatics too. It became a competition between us, to see who could discover the best new music. My mate Lewi won the competition hands down in 1986. I went round his house one day and he handed me a cassette tape. The cover was intriguing. It looked like a dead man, with his hands on his chest. It was by a band called The Smiths and the album was *The Queen is Dead*. The cover star turned out to be a French actor called Alain Delon and was taken from a 60s film called *L'insoumis*.

"Go and listen to this," he said. "What is it?" I asked. "Just listen, it's going to change your life."

I took the tape home and when my brother was out I put the tape into his stereo, put on some headphones, lay on the floor and played the album from start to finish. It wouldn't be an exaggeration to say that it blew my fucking mind. The songs were amazing. The lyrics were sublime and the musicianship unquestionable.

The 80s really was the decade of the synthesizer, but The Smiths were one of the great bands to emerge from that decade, with the traditional line up of guitar, bass and drums. I think what really appealed to me, was the juxtaposition between the often quite dark, poetic lyrics, which were accompanied by some of the most uplifting and beautiful music.

The Smiths were often labelled with the 'depressing' tag. I never saw them as depressing. There is a lot of humour present in many of The Smiths songs, but some people just didn't get it.

As strange as this may sound, if I ever feel down, I find comfort in sad music, not in happy music. If I am feeling low, I am more likely to listen to 'I Know It's Over' by The Smiths, than 'Dancing Queen' by Abba. I am not one to generalise, but I always imagined that this was the same for most people. Oh and since I just mentioned it...there is absolutely nothing wrong with a bit of Abba.

My nearest town was Wolverhampton, but it wasn't always the best place to find music, so every

Saturday, without fail, my mates and I would make the 16 mile train journey to Birmingham, and hunt down the latest vinyl. The trip wasn't the most glamorous of journeys. Wolverhampton is an industrial city in the heart of the West Midlands or the 'Black Country', as it's more popularly known, although it is often disputed as to whether Wolverhampton is actually situated within the Black Country. Anyway, Wolverhampton became wealthy in the 19th century, due to its coal and iron deposits. However, throughout the 70s and into the 80s, industry began to decline. The city's motto is, 'Out Of Darkness Cometh Light'. There wasn't any light on the train journey, just lots of black derelict factories. At the time, to me it just looked like a huge industrial wasteland. Come to think of it, I am not entirely sure much has changed.

Anyway, we would literally spend the whole day flicking through the record racks. I can recall one weekend, Lewi and I found two Smiths bootleg 7" singles in a shop called Andy's Records. They each contained four live tracks. We almost ended up fighting over them.

"I saw them first!" I said.

"Fuck off, I did," Lewi replied.

In actual fact, the conversation went a little more like this:

"I saw 'em fust!" (I saw them first.)

"Ya day!" (You didn't.)

"Yo ave 'em then, I ay bothered." (You have them then, I'm not bothered.)

I had better point out, that the West Midlands dialect can be very hard to understand.

Actually, people in Wolverhampton generally aren't that broad, compared to other parts of the West Midlands, such as Dudley. This is an example of the accent at its most unfathomable:

"I cor goo artside, cus it's rerning and I ay got naira coot!"

*Translates into*: 'I can't go outside, because it's raining and I haven't got a coat!'

Anyway, back to The Smiths. Now at that moment in time, it was my cue to stubbornly say 'No, you have them, I don't want them now.' But this was The Smiths. So I bought them. I do have to say though, when we got home, I did in fact sell one of the singles to Lewi. I had to, because he had introduced me to the band in the first place.

Lewi and I were forever arguing. We'd argue over almost anything, but most of our heated arguments were over music. We'd fall out because we'd disagree on who we thought were the best bands. We'd fall out one day, and then make up the next, just because I'd stated that Simple Minds were better than The House of Love. But that's how much it meant to us. It was our life. We lived for the music. By the way, later, my opinion was to change on that particular debate.

There was definitely an air of mystery about bands in the 1980s. It was long before the internet, so the only information you ever obtained, was through radio, music magazines like the NME and Melody Maker or the odd television appearance.

This made concerts more exciting too. Nowadays, you can view endless hours of live concert footage with the click of a mouse. It's no wonder then that in the 80s, there was a massive market for live bootleg videos. The record fairs were awash with them. People couldn't get enough live music. The dealers used to take their own VHS players and portable TVs, so you could test the quality of the video, before you parted with your hard-earned cash.

In 1987, the day finally came when I got my own stereo. It was a black Pioneer, with twin tape deck. It was my pride and joy, my own stereo, my own room, with my own music. It was amazing. All I could think about was building my own fantastic vinyl collection, I no longer had to use my brother's stereo. I hit the record fairs, the independent record stores and often swapped records with my friends. It was an amazing time, filled with a real passion for music.

I suppose now seems as good a time as any to make a confession. My brother was often suspicious that some of his vinyl had gone missing. He had so many 7" singles I just assumed that there was no way on earth he'd realise if I took a few. This was at a time, when he wasn't really playing them much anymore. That's no excuse by the way. Anyway, my friend Adrian Matthews used to come around when my brother wasn't in. He'd bring some of his records and I'd swap them for whatever he wanted of my brothers. Sorry Ian, but what can I say, I had a vinyl addiction.

I have to say though, I got caught out a few times when acquiring used records. On one occasion, my brother's friend offered to swap me his copy of The Pretenders' 7" single, 'Talk of the Town', for my copy of Captain Sensible's 'Glad It's All Over'.

I did the swap and when I got home, the record was scratched. My brother had previously shown me the technique of placing a coin on top of the record player's needle, the extra weight would sometimes allow the needle to play through small scratches. Unfortunately, the scratch was too deep. I never managed to get my record back, and was always more cautious from that moment on.

I never really analysed it much at the time. But looking back now, I really feel that music was a massive form of escapism. The West Midlands was a tough place in the seventies and eighties. I was from a working class family. My father Alan and mother Sandra both worked in a factory called GKN, which was in Bilston, a town about a mile outside my home village of Moxley, which is around 6 miles outside Wolverhampton. The streets where we lived weren't always that safe. By the way, when I say 'village', it's not to be confused with somewhere like Eton. Moxley was and is pretty much a few shops, surrounded by terraced and semi-detached houses, with a canal running alongside it. The first houses built in Moxley were for factory workers.

My mum and dad always worked hard. It must have been tough in the factory, especially for my dad who wasn't a big, strong man. He is 5'9" tall and quite thin. He never seemed to be able to put on weight for some reason, and then in 1977 all became clear, he was diagnosed with Crohn's Disease, which is an incurable inflammatory bowel disease. The main symptoms of which are abdominal pain, diarrhoea, vomiting and weight loss.

I was seven at the time, so never really understood what was going on. The one thing I did know was that my dad was very ill.

He had numerous operations to remove the parts of his bowel that were infected and had to have a colostomy procedure. An incision is made in the stomach and then the end of the large intestine is attached to the newly made incision. Your waste then passes through the intestine, out of your stomach and into a bag attached to your stomach. My dad eventually had a reversed colostomy procedure, which meant that the two ends of the bowel were reconnected.

My dad continued to work when he was well enough. He was a tool setter, so used to set up the slitting machines, which were then fed with metal. The metal was then pressed into thin sheets. The sheets would then go through a procedure which turned them into small parts used for starter motors etc, for the inside of motor cars.

My mum worked in the stores, so had to distribute the tools, as and when workers needed them. This is where my mum and dad met and fell madly in love. Their first home was a flat in Glyn Avenue, Moxley, which they moved into in 1965 and then in 1974, we moved to High Street, Moxley. It was a loving family and home felt like a safe haven.

There was a real diversity of kids living in Moxley during the eighties. Alongside the yobs, we had people like Adrian Dickson, who was amazing at table tennis and played for the county. Sisters Louise and Linda Whitehouse, who were great at languages (they eventually went to study at Oxford). Then a bunch of kids who were the same age as me, like Mick Biddulph, Craig Walton, Anthony Bailey and Paul Rennie . Mick was my best friend during my pre-teen years.

Mick and his younger brother Lyndon always got the latest toys before anyone else. I can remember him being the first kid in the street to get wireless walkie talkies. I took one over the park on a Sunday afternoon, and Mick had the other in his house, talking to me whilst he ate his dinner. I accidentally snapped the aerial off. This wasn't the

16

first toy of Mick's I had broken, genuinely by accident I might add. From that moment on, Mick's dad Brian started calling me heavy-hands.

Mick's family were like my second family really. I was always around their house as a kid. They were the first in the street to get into CB radios. They had a 40 channel Fidelity 2000 and we used to spend hours listening to Mick's mum and dad talking on it.

Moxley also attracted thugs from neighbouring areas, who would literally just hang around by our houses, most of the time just to cause trouble. There was this one guy, a punk, called Greebo, who used to just hang around our street.

His party trick was to cover one of his nostrils with a finger, then blow a boggy out of the other. He'd let it hang out his nose and then suck it back up. The guy must have had some underlying health problem, as he was always able to produce copious amounts of snot.

This was at a time when glue sniffing was rife too. I used to see used glue bags on the floor and was always genuinely perturbed by the sight. It really did scare me. I remember one occasion, walking to school along the canal. Two skinheads were sitting on a rock glue sniffing. I was terrified. I had no option but to walk past them. I just stared at the floor and increased my pace. I had my pristine school uniform on and as I walked past, one of them shouted, "We can see who's got all the money."

I wanted to say, "Yeah, my dad works his balls off in a horrible factory every day, you fucking glue sniffing loser." But of course I didn't.

Our local pub called the Moxley Arms, was right in the centre of our village, which meant we often had drunks cutting through our houses, using the route as a short cut. On one occasion, one of my best friends named Johno and me were sitting on the grassy hill, outside his house, listening to a tape of the Scottish band Big Country, on a portable cassette player. We must have only been about 14 years old, when two rough looking men walked past, and one of them muttered, "Queers!"

Listening to cassettes on the grassy hill became a real ritual. We'd listen to mix tapes or whole albums. One of the regular Sunday favourites was Clannad's album *Legend*. Released in 1984, *Legend* was the soundtrack album to the 1980s TV series *Robin of Sherwood*. A few of us were obsessed with this series.

I remember visiting my friend Sean Roberts and we got talking about Michael Praed (the actor that played Robin in the series).

Sean: "Praed is amazing. How are they going to replace him?"

Me: "Replace him? What you talking about?"

Sean: "You saw The Greatest Enemy episode didn't you?"

Me: "No!"

Sean: "Fuck, Praed's dead. He's gone mate."

Me: "Are you joking? They can't kill Praed off. Is this a joke?"

Sean: "No...he's dead. You need to see The Greatest Enemy. Sorry if I ruined it."

I couldn't believe it. Praed was gone and replaced with Jason Connery (son of Sean Connery) and the series was never the same after that. Praed left the show to join the cast of the American soap opera *Dynasty*, which probably made him a fortune. But long term, I don't think it was a great career move.

In honour of Praed, we'd often recite the

18

famous line from the series, 'Nothing is forgotten. Nothing is ever forgotten.' Fast forward to my early forties, I overheard a conversation someone was having about the Robin Hood movie which starred Kevin Costner as Robin Hood. I interrupted the conversation:

"I am sorry, there is only one Robin Hood and that's Michael Praed, end of story."

They looked at me like my lift didn't go all the way to the top floor.

Yes indeed, your childhood obsessions often stay with you for the rest of your life.

If the streets of Moxley seemed bad, the classroom at school felt even worse. I hated school, hated it with a passion. Darlaston Comprehensive School, even writing it down now gives me chills. I don't know what I feared more, the other kids or the teachers.

My first day got off to a terrible and embarrassing start. I had a sports session in the afternoon. Bearing in mind, I hated sport. I remember the games teacher Mr Morley calling out the register, when he finally got to my name:

"Davies?" he shouted.

"Yes sir."

He lifted his eyes from the register to look at me.

"Are you Ian's brother?"

"Yes sir."

"Great midfielder, your Ian was son. So we'll be signing you up for the football team then?"

"No sir," I replied.

"No, what do you mean no?" he asked.

"I've never played football sir"

"Never played football Davies? Well what do you like?"

"I like music sir."

At that point, one of my fellow pupils coughed the words "Gay sir."

I am not sure what was worse, the fact that someone called me gay, or the fact that I'd just admitted that I had never played football, in front of the entire class.

Suffice to say, games sessions went from bad to worse. At the end of our rugby sessions, anyone who wasn't dirty was thrown into a mud pool by the other kids.

This was under the teacher's orders. And yes, after every rugby session, I was indeed picked up by the whole class and thrown into the mud. My mum thought I was brilliant at rugby, as my kit was always really dirty. I did eventually tell her what was going on and she continues to repeat the story to everyone she meets to this very day. Thanks for that mum.

We also had another games teacher called Mr Jones, who used to time you whilst you got changed. If you hadn't got your top on in the allotted time, he would come behind you and smack you on the back, leaving a red mark. He called this his 'Red Hand Gang'. It only happened to me once. Believe me, once was enough. I even had to suffer yet another embarrassing moment in technical drawing class. I hadn't done my homework, so my teacher, Mr Bailey, told me that I had to endure his 'Chinese Bucket Treatment' as a punishment. This involved the teacher emptying the wastepaper bin, putting it over my head and then hitting it three times with a wooden mallet.

Schools are so different nowadays and teachers have to be really careful when they discipline the pupils. In the 80s, teachers didn't take any crap from the kids. I told my mum about the mallet incident, when I'd returned home from school and she just said, "Well that'll teach you not to do your homework."

I never really excelled academically, so as a consequence I was put in a low band, with all the hard knocks. I used to walk around the school grounds at break time, feeling totally insignificant. There were fights most days, but luckily I was never involved. I felt like I could have disappeared from class and no one would have noticed. What didn't help was the fact that the majority of my friends were younger or brighter than me, so I didn't have a single class with any of them. If I couldn't find my mates at break time, I would often seek refuge in the music block. I had started to teach myself guitar, after attempting the violin, but I wasn't very good.

The school music block was great. It was this big round building, right in the middle of the school grounds, kitted out with every kind of instrument from brass to percussion. However, there were never many pupils inside. It was always pretty empty and so you never really heard much music coming from inside. This was in complete contrast to the football field, which was always a hive of activity.

In the second year, my English teacher, Mr Clifford, kind of took me under his wing. He was a great teacher. He was quite short, stocky and had these thin rimmed glasses. I always thought he'd play a great part as Mole from *The Wind in the Willows*. He was always smiling and loved teaching.

English was the only class I genuinely enjoyed. I think Mr Clifford recognised my enthusiasm for the subject and so always encouraged me.

I loved creative writing. Again, I think it was a

form of escapism. I liked to create characters from worlds completely different to my own. You could just lose yourself in that kind of writing. It was great.

Mr Clifford even managed to rope me into starring as the Mayor of Munchkinland, in the school's production of *The Wizard of Oz*. To be honest, I didn't even have to think about it. If it meant spending less time in the playground during lunch and break time then that was fine by me. There was however, a brief moment when I thought that if I was ever going to strive for a degree of popularity in school, playing a Munchkin wasn't necessarily the right way to go about it.

Rehearsing the play was brilliant. I lost myself in it completely, plus the 6th form girl playing Dorothy was gorgeous.

We also had some of the really attractive girls from my year helping out too. I spoke to them for the first time during rehearsals, which seemed awesome to me, as I never felt confident approaching girls and I certainly wasn't cool enough to attract them. It was never really about the possibility that I may get a girlfriend. It was more about feeling like you belonged. We were all striving for the same thing. That play was my one and only positive senior school memory.

My parents came to see the play and loved it. The local newspaper did a feature on it too. I don't think they could quite believe that I actually took part. My only other performance had been starring as a wise man in the Nativity at nursery. Oh, and as part of the chorus in the scout gang show. Although this only involved standing on stage and joining in with singing 'Riding Along on the Crest of a Wave'.

My dad had been in the scouts as a child. He

always told amazing stories of camping trips and the whole camaraderie that went with being a boy scout. He eventually talked me into giving it a go. So I ended up joining 1st Bilston Scouts and loved every minute of it. To be honest, it was like I was leading a double life, because at scouts I was a totally different person. I was confident and I seemed to fit in.

On a Scout camping trip to Barmouth, Stuart Evans gave me the nickname 'Dickie', after the television sports presenter Dickie Davies. The nickname stuck. At school I was Davo and at scouts I was Dickie. I was two different people.

There were some great people in our scout troop and we did some amazing things, such as rock climbing, abseiling, trekking and camping. We once did a night hike over Long Mynd in Shropshire. The idea was to hike to the peak, then sleep over in bivvy bags and then descend the following morning. However, it was too cold, so we only spent an hour in the bags then came home.

********

From about the age of 13, I started to notice that I was becoming more and more obsessed with hygiene. At first, it was washing my hands more often than I usually would. Then things like opening doors with the sleeve of my jumper and washing my hands after handling used books and records.

Toilets became a nightmare too. I would often put reams of paper onto the toilet seat before I sat on it. Then turn my jeans up and tuck my belt in, so nothing touched the floor. It's hard to believe that the very same person, years later, could be found snorting cocaine off the top of a public toilet

23

seat.

My mates began to realise something was going on too, because I slowly began to develop another compulsion. I began staring at things on the floor. This started to happen quite regularly. It got to a point where I couldn't really hide it. We'd be outside walking along the street talking and I'd just stop in my tracks. Something would catch my eye and I'd have to stop and look at it. I'd NEVER touch it. Maybe move it with my foot, but I'd never use my hands.

It got to the point where my mates just got used to it. The thing is, they never once judged or mocked me ... ever. They'd just stand and wait for me to stop analysing whatever it was that had caught my eye, then we'd carry on as normal.

My parents were totally unaware of my issues. It is often said that during those difficult teenage years, your parents know you the least.

The worst moments were when I fought the compulsion. Lewi lived six doors away from me and sometimes when I left his house I'd run back to my front door. Something would catch my eye on the short distance back and I'd tell myself I wasn't going to stop and look at it. I'd enter my house, start to take my trainers off, but then succumb and go back outside to see what it was.

It's weird, because the hygiene issue, well that's kind of normal in a way I suppose. You can kind of rationalise that. Staring at things on the floor however, I have no idea where that came from. Part of me feels that it could have been triggered by seeing used glue bags on the ground. If ever a plastic bag caught my eye, I'd immediately think it contained glue. I'd have to check to make sure, then I'd always feel relieved if it didn't.

I was never a victim of physical bullying at

school, but I did face psychological bullying on occasions. This would sometimes be in the form of name calling or just the threat of being beaten up. Could this have been what sparked my OCD? I'm not sure.

I have always been a very sensitive person, and had an acute awareness of the fragility of my own mind. The school environment didn't suit my personality that is one thing I know for sure. Sadly, I felt like school had failed me.

I also had quite a lot of nightmares in my teens and most of them were apocalyptic in nature.

One of the worst periods was after seeing the TV programme *Threads*, which was aired on TV in 1984 and focused on the Cold War between the US and USSR. War eventually breaks out and the USSR hit a NATO base 18 miles outside Sheffield, with a nuclear warhead. The film then follows the aftermath of the attack.

I found the film terrifying at the time. I really thought there would be a war. I can even remember a teacher giving a lesson on the devastating power of nuclear weapons. When he asked if anyone had any questions, I said "Sir, will we see the bombs flying through the air?" I was the only pupil to ask a question.

My OCD gradually stopped once I'd left school. I think I just really began to relax. It was such a release knowing I'd never have to see that school or those people again. Leaving school was the best thing to happen to me. I never sought any medical help or anything like that. Perhaps because I didn't think it was taking over my life. It was certainly gone by 1990. This was the year my brother, Ian, got me a job at J.B. Makin Roofing. When you are working on a building site, you can't go and wash your hands every two minutes. And it's IMPOSSIBLE to keep your hands clean.

## Under the stars, petrol bombs and borrowing cars

By the time I had reached my final year in senior school, I was becoming more and more rebellious. In fact, I played truant for the majority of my final year. Some of my friends and I would just hang out down by the canal.

We had a cake factory in Moxley and they'd sell you cakes for 10p. Usually, they were defective cakes which they couldn't sell. The one day, I bought a huge chocolate cake and three of us were running down the street, throwing the cake to each other, when a police car came out of nowhere. "Why aren't you lot in school?" the policeman asked. "The teachers are on strike," I replied. "Well, make sure you behave yourselves." And then he just drove off. Not exactly Inspector Morse.

As far as I was concerned my mates were all good people. We never went looking for fights or anything, but we did some pretty crazy things. There was Lewi, my fellow record obsessive mate, just a year younger than me and always thought of as the leader of our group. He was super fit and great at all sports. He was 5'10" tall, with red hair, which was always cut short and neat, he was a big fan of The Jam and was always well dressed. Although he was into all sorts of music, deep down he was always a Mod. Then there was Johno, he was three years younger than me and definitely the sensible one. He was the spitting image of a young Pete Townsend from The Who. Johno and I had a shared love of martial arts. We went to karate together for a while. We were both big fans of Sho Kosugi, who was a Japanese Karate champion that went on to become a movie star in the early 80s, with films like *Enter the Ninja* and *Revenge of the Ninja*. I had already begun to collect a few martial arts weapons, such as shuriken stars and nunchaku. But then one day, for some bizarre reason, I pestered my parents for a ninja suit. I eventually got one. It was the real deal too, complete with black hood and gloves. But the question is... what do you do with a ninja suit? Moxley was hardly feudal Japan.

My parents would comment that the costume was a waste of money, as I couldn't really wear it anywhere. This got me thinking. Perhaps I could become a vigilante! I mean Moxley wasn't free from crime, in fact, far from it.

For about 2 months, after my initial brainwave, I started sneaking out, late at night, dressed as a ninja. I took my weapons too, just in case. The evening mainly involved me hiding in our tree or on top of the garages. Not exactly a healthy thing to be doing alone late at night.

The thing is, Moxley was a really rough place in the 80s and it wasn't like I could really handle myself. Plus, I'm like thirteen or something. I had one scary moment, when I almost ran into a group of drunks, returning from the Moxley Arms pub. I had to think fast and quickly hid in Mick Biddulph's garden.

Mind you, the morning's newspaper headline could have been quite funny:

'Teenage ninja ko'd by drunks on High Street, Moxley.'

I never wore the suit again after that. Plus my dad had cottoned on to the fact I was taking weapons out of the house, when they were really only supposed to be for display on my bedroom wall. The final straw came when I bought a blowpipe from Martial World in Wolverhampton. I invited a friend to come over and see it. By the time he arrived, I had made a target out of a pillow and a ZX Spectrum computer box. The blowpipe was lethal. I fired two darts, and they went straight through the pillow and right through the box.

My dad heard the thuds from the darts and the next day, dragged me to Martial World and gave the two HUGE shop owners a mouthful about the dangers of selling lethal weapons to kids. He had a point.

And then there was Jacko, who was a truly remarkable and unique individual. He did what he liked, listened to what he liked and rarely cared what anyone else thought. Also a year younger than me, he was built like a tazmanian devil, and was naturally strong. He was obsessed with drums and was a big fan of Mark Brzezicki, the amazing drummer from the Scottish band Big Country. This was the one band we all approved of.

Stuart Adamson was Big Country's founding member and a real idol to us. He had previously found success in the band Skids. Skids were often labelled as a punk band, but I always thought their music was too sophisticated to be called punk. They had some really interesting musical arrangements, not your stereotypical three chord bash. They also used synthesizers on some of their records. For a taste of Skids at their best, check out the songs, 'Woman in Winter' and 'Arena'.

Stuart Adamson played lead guitar in the Skids, but in Big Country he would take on the role as songwriter and front man, performing both vocal and guitar duties. In 1983, they released their debut album *The Crossing*, which is amazing, both musically and lyrically. Their most recognisable single taken from the album was 'Fields of Fire', which reached the top ten in the UK chart in 1983.

There was a real depth to Stuart's lyrics. He was intelligent and sensitive.

I don't know, it just kind of felt like you knew him, without having ever met him.

He was like a friend that was fighting your corner, standing up for the ordinary, working-class man.

In the booklet which accompanies the re-mastered release of Big Country's album *Steeltown*, Stuart Adamson states that the music grew out of the exploited, alienated and dispossessed.

At the end of every concert, Stuart used to tell the audience to 'Stay alive.' God, we idolised him so much. It was little known publically at the time, but he had struggled with alcoholism for a number of years. On 17th December 2001, I received a call from Lewi:

He just came out with it ... "Stuart Adamson's dead!"

"WHAT!?" I replied.

"Stuart Adamson's dead, it's been on the news."

He had hanged himself in a hotel room in Hawaii.

I was speechless for about two minutes then I hung up the phone, went upstairs, listened to the song 'Just a Shadow' from the *Steeltown* album and cried like a baby.

\*\*\*\*\*\*\*\*

Lewi, Johno and Jacko was the inner circle of friends during my post-teenage years. We were incredibly close. Then there was a broader circle, which included quite a few people, not just from Moxley, but the surrounding towns too. When we all got together, anything could happen.

Five random misadventures in no particular order:

1. Five of us decided to sleep down by the canal, to keep our friend, Gaz, company, whilst he was night fishing. It was a glorious night under the stars but it was really cold and we couldn't sleep, so three of my mates went off wondering the streets of Moxley to try and get warm. About an hour later, they returned with a jerry can full of petrol and glass milk bottles. They had siphoned the petrol from cars parked in the street. I have no idea where they got the jerry can from, or the rubber pipe to siphon the petrol. Anyway, one of my mates poured a trail of petrol leading to Gaz's fishing tackle, then lit a match and dropped it! There was a huge whoosh, the petrol ignited and in a flash Gaz's fishing box was on fire. Mass panic broke out and we all tried to put out the flames with jackets and dirt, we just about managed to keep it under control and salvaged the fishing tackle.
If that wasn't bad enough, we then began to fill the empty milk bottles with petrol, to make petrol bombs. We then proceeded to light the bombs and randomly throw them at a nearby factory wall.

2. Lewi's older brother had two air rifles and occasionally we would take them without him knowing. One day we took them down to the canal and decided to play armies. Lewi hid behind one side of the canal bridge and me the other. We then began shooting at each other. Luckily neither of us got shot. A miracle really, considering we were less than 50 metres away from each other. I don't think a life in the military was ever going to be a

31

career option.

3. Between the ages of about 14 to 16, I had taught myself to drive. My brother was already an employee of J.B. Makin Roofing Contractors Ltd. He used to bring the work's van home and leave it out the back of our house. Now, on a Sunday, my brother used to play football. He'd then go for a drink with his mates, leaving the van keys on his bedside table. So......I used to take the keys and attempt to drive the van.

It started with me driving forward a few feet, then finding reverse and driving back a few feet. This went on for quite a few weeks, until it gradually progressed to taking the van for a spin around the block. Then eventually, I was taking friends for drives around the streets of Moxley.
This leads neatly onto number4.

4. Lewi's parents had 2 cars. A Volkswagen Golf and a Mini. One night, I was home alone, when Lewi turned up at my door. He told me that his parents had gone for a ride out in the country in their Mini.
   Lewi was waving a set of keys in my face. They were the keys to his parents' Volkswagen Golf.
"I've got my dad's keys, let's go and pick Jacko up."
"Great," I replied.
Then off we drove to Jacko's house. Jacko grabbed his coat and came running up to the car. Without a second thought, he lay down spread eagle on the bonnet and shouted "drive!"
So I did. I drove about 100 meters with Jacko holding onto the bonnet for dear life. I stopped and then he climbed into the car and we drove off

laughing.

Just outside Moxley was a big industrial estate, I drove there, knowing it would be fairly quiet. I stopped the car at the top of the estate, and began to rev the engine. I quickly released the clutch and we sped down the road, gradually increasing in speed.

We eventually hit 65 mph, when we reached the end of the road. Lewi called out, "Do it again."

Before I could turn around to drive back up the road, a police car just appeared out of nowhere. It was like the shopkeeper from the early 70s cartoon, called *Mr Benn*. The series was about a man who lived at 52 Festive Road. Every episode, he would visit a fancy dress shop and pick a costume, he would then walk through a magic door and be sent on a fantastic adventure, related to the particular costume he had tried on.

I loved the series, but always wanted him to go on a space adventure, or pick an army outfit and go into battle. Whenever I watched it though, I always seemed to catch the boring episodes where he chose a cook outfit, or became a zoo-keeper.

Anyway, at the end of the adventure, the shopkeeper used to appear from out of nowhere and take Mr Benn back to the costume shop. There was usually a moral to the tales and there was certainly a moral to mine.

Having a police car right behind you with its flashing lights on at night, is a terrifying experience. The flashing lights completely engulfed the inside of our car and the noise from the siren was piercing.

I started to drive away.

Lewi screamed out, "Fucking hell we are in the shit now.'"

"Shall I try and outrun them?" I replied.

Jacko was constantly yelling, "Fuck, fuck, fuck!"
Lewi had the final say ... "Just pull over."
So I did.

The policeman took me to the police car, leaving Lewi and Jacko in the Volkswagen.

"Will I have to go to court?" I asked.

"Yes," replied the officer, without any emotion whatsoever.

After answering all the officer's questions, such as age, address and who the owner of the car was etc, the officer's colleague drove Lewi's parents' car home, with us all in it. However, because our parents weren't home, it was left to us to break the news.

I hated that feeling you had in the pit of your stomach, when you had done something wrong and had to tell your parents. I'd usually refrain from telling them for as long as I possibly could. I had, however, begun to realize that this just prolongs the agony. So for that reason alone, I decided to tell them as soon as they walked through the door.

Me: "I've been arrested."

Dad: "What do you mean, you've been arrested?"

Me: "We took Lewi's dad's car for a drive and the police caught us."

Mum: "I'm going to bed." She had no words of comfort.

At this point I'm expecting my dad to go ballistic.

Dad, calm as anything, "Well ... it's your mistake and you'll pay for it, I'm off to bed."

And that was that! I had so made the right decision not to sleep on it.

I eventually went to court, had a £220 fine and 6

penalty points on a driving licence that I didn't even have yet.

5. My mates and I had a very unhealthy obsession with fireworks. I discovered, that if you took a thin piece of plastic drainpipe about 2 feet long, covered the one end with sellotape and then poured about 2 inches of sand inside, that you had a homemade rocket launcher.

We used to get the older lads to buy us packs of 10 mini rockets. One of us would then hold the drainpipe, whilst someone else would light the rocket and slide it down the tube.

You'd then aim it at something, which was usually our local block of flats. The idea was to try and get the right distance between you and the building, so that the rocket would explode as it hit the windows.

********

It's fair to say, that I was in danger of becoming just as bad as all the other Moxley yobs. They were constantly getting into trouble. However, my trip to court was enough of a shock to make me realise I didn't want to go back there ever again. This coupled with the fact that I had started dating a girl. Her name was Jayne Southall-Owen. She was from Ettingshall, Wolverhampton.

Jayne was a massive music fan too. Her dad, Harry, had been a singer in various bands and would take his family with him whenever he was performing. In fact, Jayne had started going to concerts a few years before me. She went with her best friend, Alison Jones to see Big Country at the NEC in 1985. They were only 14 years old at the time.

Lewi didn't really approve of Jayne. I think he thought she'd drive a wedge between us. And I suppose to a certain degree she did, because as time went on I was spending a lot less time with Lewi.

I had met Jayne at scouts of all places. Which is very unusual, considering the fact that scouts was a boys only club. However, Jayne and Alison had managed to blag themselves on a few of our camping trips. Alison's brother was one of the most respected scouts and would often get the girls involved in various scout trips and fetes etc.

Actually, thinking about it, if I remember correctly, I actually fell asleep and dribbled on Jayne's shoulder, after our Long Mynd night hike. This was a few years before we actually got together.

Jayne even managed to get me into football. Like my own family, Jayne's were all football fanatics too. Her dad and two brothers, Paul and Andrew, all support Wolverhampton Wanderers. What really surprised me was that Jayne possessed an almost encyclopaedic knowledge of football history.

Even to this day, I think people are genuinely surprised at how knowledgeable Jayne is on the 'beautiful game'. Anyway, I was gradually brainwashed by Jayne and her family and I could resist no longer. I became a fully-fledged supporter of Wolverhampton Wanderers.

Both my Dad and brother were really surprised, as they had never been able to get me to follow football throughout my youth. In fact, I can remember on one occasion, I must have been about 10 years old. My brother had *Match of the Day* on the TV, but was reading a newspaper at the same time. I hated football, so told him to change the channel. He wouldn't do it. I told him that he couldn't read the newspaper and watch TV at the same time. He told me that he could, so I got off the sofa, grabbed the newspaper and punched him in the face. He then chased me into the kitchen, tripped me up and started hitting me. My dad had to pull my brother off me.

My dad dragged me to a few games around the late seventies. He'd take a little wooden folding stool, so I could stand on it to see. He'd take me into the south bank stand. However, I just couldn't get into it.

It was a different story for my brother. He was a football nut. He was a spectator and a player. And to be so well remembered by his sports teacher, well I guess my brother must have made a real impression on the school football field.

It's a big regret for me now, the fact that I never played football. I think about it a lot as I get older. It would have been great to be in the school football team. Our school had pedigree too, as it produced a professional footballer; Scott Green, he was in my year at school, he went on to play for Bolton Wanderers. Impressive...oh and I once got to see him score against Wolverhampton Wanderers at the Molineux Stadium.

### Pat-a-cake, pat-a-cake, baker's man

After leaving school in 1986 and having no real job prospects, the obvious next step was college. I enrolled on two courses at Bilston Community College, English and computing. I thought I might like computing, purely because I had owned a Sinclair ZX Spectrum and enjoyed playing video games.

I hated computing! My lecturer looked like the British actor Roddy McDowell, who was most famous for his role as Cornelius in the late 60s, early 70s film series of *Planet of the Apes*. He was a nice bloke, but his teaching technique wasn't very exciting. But then again, how can you breathe life into teaching Pascal computer programming language? This was still the eighties, so all the printers in the class were dot matrix. These printers used ink ribbons, so they were a similar mechanism as a typewriter. The thing is, you could never read the print outs properly, and all our work was done on them. I just couldn't be bothered. It all seemed like too much effort.

I eventually left the college and started to look for work. I really did feel worthless at this point in my life. I applied for so many jobs. I got that desperate I even applied for a job cleaning a pub. At the interview, I was asked if I had any experience. I said that I often cleaned my mum's house. That was a lie. Suffice to say I didn't get the job.

I bumped into a mate in the street one day. He said he'd got a job at the local bakery, situated on the outskirts of Moxley. Mr. Crusty. He said they'd take anyone on. I said, "Really? What, they'd even take me, with my limited knowledge of computer programming and inability to mop a floor." He got me an interview, I got the job and I was finally off unemployment benefit.

My general bakery duties involved making the bread and cake mix. The bread mix was put into big machines, which cut the dough into pieces and moulded it into cobs. The cobs came out the front of the machine on a conveyor belt. You then had to put the cobs onto trays, ready to go into the oven for baking.

Mr. Crusty was located in quite an odd place. Moxley was one side of the canal and the bakery was on the other side. However, it was so close to the canal that you'd occasionally get a rat run across the factory floor. I once told a colleague that he should play for the England football team; one day I was busy making cobs, when all of a sudden I heard a loud voice cry "RAT!" As I turned around one of the workers just ran towards this big furry rodent, which was scuttling along the floor and swung his right foot David Beckhamesque. It was a direct hit and the rat flew across the factory floor and hit the wall. It was dead as a doornail. He picked it up by the tail and put it in the bin.

On one occasion, there was a big announcement. We were told that Mr. Crusty was about to receive a new fleet of vans. We were told to prepare ourselves, as the logo on the vans was going to really blow our minds. I didn't know what to expect. I remember thinking that it must be something really cool, the way management were going on and on about it. A graffiti style logo or something really eye catching, like a 3 dimensional holographic image. None of the workers really cared to tell the truth.

It's fair to say, that no one could have predicted

what we were about to see. The vans finally arrived and all the workers were escorted out of the bakery en masse.

The sight with which we were greeted was unbelievable. The vans contained a huge mural, which featured a depiction of the feeding of the 5000. In the picture, Jesus was behind a rock talking into a telephone. The speech bubble that was coming from Jesus' mouth said, 'Quick, get me Mr. Crusty!'

As I said, Mr. Crusty was right next to a canal. It was also next to a church. The amount of complaints the company received was incredible. Mr Crusty was accused of blasphemy. Within a month, the vans were sent off to have the murals removed.

Although the job itself was really monotonous, we did have some good laughs. Mr Crusty really did employ some bizarre characters.

The foreman would constantly be on your back shouting "Come on, come on, quicker, get the bloody mixer switched on. Martin, where's that cake mix?" I would mutter the famous nursery rhyme to myself "Pat-a-cake, pat-a-cake baker's man, bake me a cake as fast as you can."

About once a week, I'd have the privilege of jamming doughnuts. Believe me, after making cobs and bread rolls all day, this felt like a promotion. I invented a funny way of amusing myself. Once the doughnuts were baked, you had a portable jamming machine. It contained two spikes, both of which had a handle, then underneath the handle was a bowl, this contained the jam. You'd have a tray full of freshly baked doughnuts, you'd take two, push them onto the spikes then you'd push the handles down twice, pump, pump. Then you'd dip them in a bowl containing sugar.

Same again, onto the spikes, pump, pump, sugar.

Two more, pump, pump, sugar.

Pump, pump, sugar.

Pump, pump, sugar.

Pump, pump, sugar.

Pump, pump, sugar.

So, you get the idea right?

Now, my little game was:

Pump, pump, pump, pump, pump, pump sugar.

Pump, pump, pump, pump, pump, pump sugar.

Four extra pumps meant a LOT more jam. I did this, purely in the hope that some unsuspecting customer would bite into the doughnut and get covered in jam. It kept me amused for a while anyway.

Some of the factory machinery was so old, that half the time the safety guards didn't work. It's a miracle no one had a serious accident. The safety guard automatically switches the machine off, if something larger than dough goes through it, such as a hand. Underneath the guards were two metal rollers that would have no problem crushing bones.

A lot of our products went to Birmingham International Airport. I remember turning up for work one morning, when the foreman gathered all the workers on the shop floor. He produced a mini-loaf of bread, which had been returned from the airport.

"Can anyone tell me what's been found inside this?" he asked.

No one answered. We just all stood looking

perplexed.

"Well? No one got an answer?"

Still there was silence.

He shouted at the top of his voice "THIS WAS FUCKING FOUND INSIDE!" He then produced a razor blade.

I thought, shit, someone is definitely getting sacked over this. I couldn't believe it. Now I have to point out, that razor blades were common in the bakery, as they were often used to put cuts into the batch loaves, but a lot of the work's blades didn't even have the trade mark bright red handle. They were literally just razor blades. It was so dangerous. You'd put requests in for new blades or oven gloves etc and they'd never arrive. It was such a mickey mouse company.

No one lost their job, as it was impossible for the foreman to find out who was responsible. There is every chance that it was purely and simply an accident.

My best friend at work was Andy Muckley. He had been a drummer in a rock band called Requiem. They'd even had an independent record deal, which I found super impressive.

Andy played me a live recording they had made and his drumming was awesome. At one point Andy had a big drum solo, and the lead singer shouted into the microphone "Andy Muckley on the drums!" and the crowd went crazy.

Andy was a big rock fan and one of his favourite bands was an American band called Journey. Their most well-known song was a track called 'Don't stop Believin'. He knew I was heavily into electronic music, but never mocked me. He was just happy that he'd got a work colleague, that was as obsessed about music as he was. We were both really into visiting record fairs and buying record collector magazine, but we never went to record fairs together. If there was a local fair and he couldn't make it, he'd write me a list of vinyl he wanted. I'd take it with me and do my best to track down as many of the records as I could find.

It's funny, because I wrote him a list once and it contained records by Depeche Mode and Erasure. He visited a record fair on the Saturday and came to work on the Monday, with a rare 7" Erasure single and the holy grail of Erasure 12" singles, the rare 'Heavenly Action (Yellow Brick Mix)'.

I just wondered what the dealer must have thought, seeing this rocker with long hair purchasing an Erasure record. That still amuses me. How brilliant though, that he'd do that for me. Andy always was a top man.

Erasure were never considered cool. I didn't care though. I always rated Vince Clarke as a bloody good songwriter. He had previously been the main songwriter in Depeche Mode. But after the first album *Speak and Spell*, I think he got tired of running his songs past the other band members. I think he thought he could do it all on his own, which of course he did. After leaving Depeche Mode, he recruited Alison Moyet on vocals and formed Yazoo and then later found even greater success with the vocalist Andy Bell, under the name Erasure.

Andy Bell grabbed so much attention, especially during live performances, because he was so openly gay and often wore the most outrageous costumes. He'd wear things like angel wings or leotards. At one concert, he had tinsel covering his genitalia.

The remarkable thing was, rather than deciding to split up, having lost their main songwriter, Depeche Mode decided to soldier on, with Martin

Gore attempting to take on the role as chief songwriter. Martin would lead the band down a much darker musical pathway and by the time they had released their 1986 classic *Black Celebration* album, they had pretty much cemented themselves as my favourite band of all time. I joined the fan club and bought everything they ever released, including 7" singles, 12" singles, remixes and imports.

People often think that Depeche Mode are a niche, cult band, however, they have sold over 100 million records worldwide. I don't think there are that many electronic 80s bands that have reached anywhere near that amount of sales.

On the subject of Erasure, I remember telling Mark, one of the Mr Crusty foremen, that I was going to see Erasure at the National Exhibition Centre.

Mark was well over 6ft tall and had done a stint in the army. In fact, he ran the weekend shifts like a military operation. He'd say stuff like, "Right men, when I call your name, say yes sergeant." Only really messing about, but I found it really amusing and so went along with it.

"Davies?" he'd shout.

"Yes sergeant."

"Is the bread ready Davies?"

"Not yet sergeant."

"What's the ETA on the bread Davies?"

"10 minutes sergeant."

"Understood Davies, keep up the good work."

"Yes sergeant."

The bakery owners weren't in on a Sunday, so Mark used to instigate flour fights. This sounds quite harmless, but believe me, if you get flour in your eyes, you know about it. On one particular day, I was hiding behind an oven during one of the flour fights. I popped my head around the oven to see if anyone was coming, when I just saw this massive white cloud of flour travelling at speed towards my face. I was temporarily blinded. It completely dried my eyes.

Someone pulled me to the sink and began throwing water over my face. It took me two days to get over it. I thought it might have permanently damaged my eyes.

Anyway back to Mark.

He said, "Will you bring me an Erasure t shirt from the concert?"

"Of course," I said. I didn't even know he was a fan.

"What colour do you want?" I asked.

"Whatever they've got will be fine, just make sure it's an extra-large."

That much I did know. He was a big bloke.

So I went to the concert and before the show, I visited the merchandise stall. They had lots of different t-shirt designs. I bought Mark and me a t-shirt featuring the album cover of their latest LP, *The Innocents*. I also bought myself a white Erasure vest. I have no idea why I bought it at the time, because to say it looked camp, was an understatement. It was ultra slim fit.

I wondered to myself what my old games teacher Mr. Morley would have thought, had he seen me trying it on.

Incidentally, the concert was filmed for VHS release. At one point I can be seen swinging my t-shirt above my head, about five rows from the front of the stage.

When I returned to work, Mark was suitably impressed with his t-shirt. I was still genuinely surprised that he wanted one in the first place. He asked me what I'd bought for myself, at this point

I felt a little nervous. Do I tell him about the vest? The big ex-military man, would he think that an Erasure vest was a step too far? Would I again be inviting ridicule? Anyway, I just came out with it:

"I bought a t shirt and … a vest."

"A vest!" Mark shouted, "a vest!"

In a slight panic, I replied, "Yeah, I just thought it might be good for the summer, to keep cool." I was desperately trying to justify my purchase, when Mark shouted:

"Why didn't you get me a bloody vest!?"

The mind boggles.

I have to also point out, that even Andy Muckley ended up getting into Erasure. He really rated *The Innocents* album and had it playing in his car for months.

I never did get into Journey though.

## Are Friends Electric?

Over the years, my brother had bombarded my ears with so much electronic music, it was inevitable that it was going to have indelible effect on me, and synthesizers started to become a real obsession. How on earth were people creating these amazing sounds? Gary Numan, Depeche Mode, Kraftwerk. Who were these people? Where did they come from? What equipment were they using? It was like an impenetrable world, a mysterious world, I could never be part of. I had tried to play guitar and violin at school, but synthesizers were different ... they were super cool.

It wasn't until Christmas 1988, that I actually ended up owning a keyboard. My girlfriend surprised me with a Yamaha PSR home keyboard. I was blown away to be honest. I had these grand visions of playing 'Are Friends Electric' by Gary Numan. However, when I plugged the keyboard in, my heart sank. I had forgotten one fundamental thing, the fact that I had no idea how to play the thing.

If I was going to take the keyboard seriously, then I was going to need some lessons. I decided to attend group keyboard lessons, at a music school in Wolverhampton.

I enjoyed this for a while and certainly picked up the basics, however, I was itching to start a band. My friend Lewi had started to learn guitar and our mutual love of music led us to become a duo. We started to write songs and for the first time, I actually began to realise that this is how other bands must have started. Perhaps the music industry might not be so impenetrable after all.

I always had big ambitions and although playing music with mates was great, I wanted to push myself even more. I remember seeing an ad in the newspaper. A local rock band called, Sahara Darc were seeking a keyboard player, so I decided to audition. I travelled on the bus, with the Yamaha home keyboard under my arm and made my way up the flight of stairs to the Attic studio's rehearsal room in Bilston. Upon my arrival, I could see that the band possessed a ton of equipment. The drum kit was huge, the guitars and amps all looked really expensive and here was me, with my £250 Yamaha home keyboard. It was intimidating.

The band consisted of Al Barrow on bass, his brother Rob on drums and Carl Jones on guitar. The band was also looking for a new vocalist. I think Rob and Al's sister had been the original singer. Anyway, the band was really professional. They had obviously been together for some time. I was so nervous and I knew the audition wasn't going to be easy.

Al asked me, "What songs do you know?"

"Well...I know some Gary Numan, Orchestral Manoeuvres in the Dark and Depeche Mode."

I had also learnt the whole of Vangelis' 'Chariots of Fire', but I didn't mention this.

Everyone stared at me blankly. It was a tumbleweed moment.

"We don't really play that kind of music," said Rob.

"Eeerrrmmm...oh, I know how to play 'Jump' by Van Halen."

There was an outburst of enthusiasm.

Al: "Oh, great."

Rob: "Ok, let's play 'Jump', ready, on four, 1,

2..."

Me: "hang on, hang on ... I need to find a keyboard sound!"

Unfortunately, my keyboard didn't have a sound even remotely close to the one used on the Van Halen track, so I ended up using a sound called 'Rock Organ'.

The band played the song like they'd been doing it all their lives. The guitarist even played the guitar solo, note for note. The band could really play, I mean REALLY play. Suffice to say, I couldn't recreate the synthesizer solo. But I had managed to blag my way through to the end of the song.

I didn't think I had any chance of getting in the band, but I guess they saw something in me, because they said they'd let me join on the understanding that I invested in a professional keyboard as soon as possible. So I kept saving my money and eventually bought a Kawai K1 synthesizer. I had finally acquired my very first professional keyboard. I knew it was the real deal because it didn't have a built in speaker, that's exactly how I judged the worth of a synthesizer at that particular time. If it needed separate amplification, it was professional.

The Kawai served me well. It could be quite limiting playing with just one synthesizer, but the Kawai allowed you to split the keyboard up into zones. So for instance, you could assign, say strings to the lower end of the keyboard and a brass sound to the upper part of the keyboard, thus giving you much more flexibility to your playing.

I really began to grow more and more confident with my ability, and before long I was bringing my own compositions to the rehearsals. We would then, as a band, turn them into full songs. It was really rewarding.

The big downside to joining Sahara Darc was that Lewi treated me like a pariah and I lost touch with him for a good few years. This really hurt my feelings. But I just couldn't detract from my tunnel vision, which was to play keyboards in a professional band.

The guys in the band were so nice and they were great musicians. Ok, it was rock, which wasn't really my bag, but they did help me develop as a player. I have nothing but fond memories of that band. Plus, they had taken a chance on me, with my very limited ability. I will always be grateful.

It's funny, because years later, in 1997, I was at university and working a temporary Christmas job at Argos, in Wolverhampton. I had heard that Al Barrow had joined a new band, called Hard Rain. This was basically the core members of the rock band Magnum, whose 1988 album *Wings of Heaven* had gone silver with 200,000 sales in the UK.

Anyway, one Saturday afternoon in Argos, who happens to walk through the doors? Al Barrow. I thought, 'Shit. He's touring the world and I am stuck in Argos.' I wondered whether I'd be able to hide from him, behind the mass of toys people were buying for Christmas. Impossible, it was just too busy to stop working. To make matters even worse, Al had to collect his purchase from my bloody collection point.

"Alright Mart, how are you doing?" he asked.

"I am ok thanks Al, how about you?"

"I am great thanks."

I couldn't resist asking about his new band, the curiosity just got the better of me.

"I hear you are working with the Magnum guys' new band."

"Yes mate, I cannot believe it, it feels like I have won the lottery."

He continued to explain how fantastic it all was. I was just standing there, wondering how good his life must be. Touring, recording etc, then he was gone.

I didn't really have much time to dwell on the conversation, because before he'd even left the building, I heard the loud automated voice say, "Order number 242, to your collection point please." And it was back to work.

I left Sahara Darc in 1990 to join a psychedelic/indie band, called Sunny Daze.

It was a sad day really. The lads were disappointed that I was leaving the band, I was too, but I saw the move as a possible chance for me to make strides towards the end game … a record deal.

This also coincided with a change of job too. My brother got me a job at J.B. Makin Roofing Ltd.

Sunny Daze came from Wolverhampton and had recently recorded a demo tape. The opening track was called 'I Don't Know Why', and was really reminiscent of the song 'The Only One I Know' by The Charlatans. The lead singer was a guy called Steve Moxon, who had a fantastic voice. Not only that, but he looked great too. The first time I met him, was at a band rehearsal at Sneyd School, in Bloxwich. He had a baggy t shirt on, a beaded necklace and shades. I just remember thinking, 'Fuck, this guy is a star!'

I really believed that Sunny Daze could achieve something special. The band had some really commercial songs. Not only that, but they had a manager too.

The manager's name was Paul Cook and he looked just like the actor, Danny Devito, so much so, I swear they could be twins (pardon the pun). He wasn't a full time music manager. He had a furniture shop in Bridge Street, Walsall. This was quite handy, because Paul used to let us use a space at the back of his shop, as our rehearsal room.

Paul Cook really believed in the band, and he worked hard to get us gigs and generate interest within the music industry. He once got us a support with Ocean Colour Scene in Liverpool, although that very nearly ended in disaster. Midway through our set, Steve Moxon decided to roll across the stage screaming into the microphone, Jim Morrison style. He'd never done anything like this before and after the show, we had to hold our lead guitarist Paul Martin back, to stop a potential fight.

"If he does that again, I'm fucking leaving the band!" screamed Paul.

We managed to gain a good local following and once put on a coach trip, to take our fans to see us play live at a new indie night, called 'Butterfly Evolution', which was being held at the Carnarvon Castle, on Chalk Farm Road, London. Our fans just about got there in time, because the coach got lost in central London. Our manager's wife was trying to give directions, but they didn't prove to be that accurate, and the coach ended up going round in circles.

Sunny Daze did have a lot of record label interest, we had A&R from Virgin Records come and see us supporting The Field Mice at The Dome in London. We also had interest from ZTT records, which was a label set up by NME journalist Paul Morley and producer Trevor Horn.

We used to have regular meetings at the manager's house and he'd inform us on all the latest developments. At a meeting in 1991, he told us that Hut Records were really interested in signing us, but that they could only make so many signings a year and were also showing interest in another band called Verve. Suffice to say, Hut Records never did sign Sunny Daze, but opted to sign Verve instead and the rest as they say, is history.

We once had a gig at The Cavern Club in Liverpool. Someone had roped in an ex-policeman to be our roady and driver. Once I set eyes upon this chap, I would NEVER have guessed he'd been in the police force. He looked like the singer/songwriter Julian Cope, both in his facial features and his hair, which was a bit wild and reminiscent of Julian's hair on the *World Shut Your Mouth* album cover. He was wearing this dirty t shirt with holes in and dungarees. I am not sure he was all the ticket to be honest.

We were in the van on the M6 motorway, travelling up to Liverpool, when I decided to play a game with my band mates. I took a box of matches and made a hole in the box with a match. I then told the guys they had to do this with one hand ... I took a match out of the box, pushed the match into the hole I had made, then took another match out of the box, struck that match and then lit the match that was sticking out of the box ...all with just using one hand. Then Paul Cashmore, our bass player attempted it. Suddenly a shout came from the front of the van. "I wanna try, let me try." It was our ex-plod roady. "You can't, you are driving," I replied.

"Right, I am not touching this steering wheel until you give me the matches." Then he let go of the steering wheel! I screamed, "Give him the fucking matches." I grabbed them off Cash and threw them at him. He managed to complete the match game, whilst doing 60mph on the motorway.

In early 1992, a local newspaper printed an article with the headline: 'Local band have music industry in a real Daze'. It mentioned all the record labels that were showing interest in us. I really believed we were going to get signed, I think we all did. The newspaper came to one of our rehearsals and took a picture to accompany the article. In the picture, you can just about make out the plaster on my right foot, from my roofing accident.

We never did get our hands on that elusive recording contract and by early 1993 I was becoming really disillusioned with Sunny Daze. The singer's behaviour was becoming more and more erratic. You were always wondering what he was going to do next. The whole situation came to a head at a gig at the legendary JB's in Dudley.

JB's was one of the Midland's most renowned music venues. During its history, it had played host to the likes of U2, Blur, The Stone Roses and also, purveyors of the local 'Stourbridge' music scene with the likes of Ned's Atomic Dustbin, Pop Will Eat Itself and The Wonder Stuff.

I arrived at the venue and started unloading my keyboards, when Paul Martin, our guitarist came up to me and asked,

"Have you seen Steve yet?"

"No," I replied, "why?"

"Wait until you see him."

I walked through the stage door of the venue and there was Steve, sound checking on the microphone. I couldn't quite believe what I was seeing. Steve had shaved off all his hair and had painted a diamond on his forehead. I knew that was the beginning of the end.

Eventually, Sunny Daze replaced Steve with a female vocalist named Kirstie Bailey, and the band changed its name to Kill Toto. Kirstie was very a good singer, but it did change the dynamic and sound of the band. Later, whenever Paul Cook spoke to the record labels that had been keeping an eye on us, they weren't really interested in the band any longer, they just kept saying, "Let us know when Steve Moxon has a new band."

My last hoorah with Kill Toto came in 1993 with a brilliant acoustic show at Wolverhampton's Connaught Hotel. Local promoter Markus Sargeant had been putting on these fantastic shows. He'd booked the likes of David Gray and the amazing Jeff Buckley.

Our manager Paul Cook rang me and asked if I was sitting down. I was expecting bad news or something, but then he proceeded to tell me that we would be supporting Brian Kennedy and The Fat Lady Sings at the Connaught Hotel.

This was massive news for me, as I was a big fan of both these artists.

The Fat Lady Sings were from Dublin. I had seen them live a couple of years earlier, supporting Hothouse Flowers and they were amazing. Their debut album *Twist* was released in 1991 on East West Records and I played it non-stop at the time.

Brian Kennedy was from Belfast. I had first seen him singing live on television, around the release of his debut album *The Great War of Words* in 1990. In my opinion, that album still stands the test of time and should be given 'classic' status.

As it was an acoustic show, we didn't play with full band. It was just Paul Martin on acoustic guitar, Kirstie on vocals and me on electric piano.

It was an epic night. There were no egos, just great people playing great music.

After Kill Toto, I started to lose the love of playing live. I'd also lost touch with all my childhood friends and that played on my mind, because they'd been such a big part of my life growing up. But then, during the tail end of 1993, I had a chance meeting with Lewi's older brother. He told me that Lewi, Jacko and Johno had started a band and were recording material. It didn't surprise me really, as they had always been music fanatics, and had an inseparable bond ever since childhood.

Their band was called Twister. It consisted of Lewi on vocals and guitar, Johno on bass guitar and Jacko on drums. To cut a long story short, Lewi ended up talking me into joining the band. However, they didn't want a keyboard player, so he suggested I join on bass guitar and he said that Johno could switch between lead guitar and rhythm guitar. I thought the idea was crazy. I'd never played a bass guitar before. However, Lewi had faith in me:

"Give it a go. You used to play guitar for a while, bass is easier."

"Yeah, but you are all sorted as a unit. I will just hold everything up attempting bass guitar."

"There's no timeline, just try it. Imagine the four of us back together. We'll have a great time."

"But you know what I'm like. I can't go on stage as an average bass player. Johno is great on bass. I am not sure I can be that good."

"Fuck it, just try."

"Ok, I'll give it a go."

I kept thinking about all the great bass players that utilised the bass as a lead instrument, Peter Hook from New Order, Mick Karn from Japan. I wanted to be as good as them, but deep down I knew that I wouldn't be. But, I would be playing alongside my childhood friends and that in itself was worth a lot.

Of course, we'd have disagreements, but when you know people that well you never really take anything personally. It's the most fun I've ever had playing music. We were like a gang.

My friend Keith Berridge managed Twister for a while. My wife and I had met Keith and his wife Ann in Dublin 1989. My wife was a big U2 fan and as a Christmas present that year, I got her tickets to see the band's show at The Point Depot, as part of their Lovetown Tour. The show was on 30th December and we travelled by coach which departed from outside the Grand Theatre, Wolverhampton.

Keith once told me, that when he saw me get on the coach he told his wife that I was trying to be a Larry Mullan (U2's drummer) lookalike. I wasn't even a fan of U2! However, there was an uncanny resemblance, in that I had the same colour hair, greased back and a tight leather biker jacket and boots. Anyway, we later became close friends. Keith had played drums in a three-piece band called Boiling Over and I attended a couple of their rehearsals with my keyboard. I can remember playing covers of Eric Clapton's 'Wonderful Tonight' and U2's 'New year's Day.'

The Mod scene came back in a big way during the mid-nineties, and this certainly influenced our image and music. Our stage wear would often include corduroy trousers, Fred Perry polo shirts and desert boots.

We also shared a love of classic bands like The Small Faces, The Who, The Kinks and The Beatles. Mind you, I could never profess to be as big a fan of The Beatles as Lewi, because he was obsessed with them.

I would often wear eyeliner onstage. We did one show at the Wolverhampton University Ball, which was being held at Dudley Castle, when a girl in the audience recognised me and came to the front of the stage after the show. I was expecting her to compliment on how good we'd been, but she said, "Why are you wearing eyeliner?" So I just replied, "Because I'm in touch with my feminine side."

I assume that because we had a mod image, people just thought I had stolen the idea of wearing eye liner from the character of Jimmy, in The Who's 1979 mod film *Quadrophenia*. However, it was more to do with the fact that I had a slight obsession with men in make-up. Not in a sexual way, more the idea of taking on a different persona.

Recently, Mick Biddulph sent Wayne Stokes and me an email, asking if we remember doing a routine to David Bowie's 'Space Oddity' at junior school.

Apparently, the routine was entered into some sort of competition and we got into a fight with some rival school kids who picked on us in the toilets for wearing make-up.

Now, I remember the rehearsals for the show quite vividly, but I have no recollection of the competition itself, or the fight. It made me smile though, the thought that there were junior school boys picking fights with other boys, just because they were wearing make-up.

Twister were guilty of some very hit and miss

shows. During one show at First Base in Wolverhampton, I had danced so much, that halfway through the set, I was too exhausted to carry on and collapsed on the stage. The band just carried on playing and finished the set without me.

Another time, we were travelling to Birmingham to play a show at the Flapper and Firkin. We had gone in two cars, with all our gear in the back. Johno and Jacko were in the car ahead of us, when we both got caught at a set of traffic lights. Lewi and me, were sticking our fingers up at them, giggling like children. Right next to our car was a huge lorry and when the lights changed to green, the lorry rammed my car off the road. We actually mounted the pavement. If anyone had been walking past, they could have been killed. We just sat there looking at each other stunned, for about 5 minutes. "What the fuck just happened?" asked Lewi. "I dunno," I replied. "The lorry driver must have thought we were sticking our fingers up at him," I said.

The lorry had long gone, so we didn't get his registration number. We just carried on to the venue in my newly dented car and played the show.

I had taken it upon myself to send out demo tapes to venues and music industry personnel. I enjoyed the kind of managerial role really and it was always exciting when a venue got back to you with a booking. I had a real surprise one day, when Neil Burrow, the manager of The Bluetones phoned my parents' house, asking for me. I was so nervous.

The Bluetones had released their debut album *Expecting to Fly* in 1996 and it had gone to number 1 in the UK. It had been helped along by their fantastic single, 'Slight Return' which peaked

59

at number 2.

Neil said, "I really like your demo, have you got anymore material recorded?"

"We are just about to record a new demo," I replied.

"Can you send me a copy when it's finished? You've got a great sound."

"Absolutely, I will send it straight over when it's been mixed. Thanks a lot.'

I couldn't wait to tell the other band members. It put us all on such a high. Could this be it? The moment we had all been waiting for. With Neil Burrow on board, we would surely get a record deal.

And then ... back down to earth with a bang. The high was short lived. We sent Neil our newly recorded tracks and never heard from him again.

## Speed freaks and self-harm

Being off work for eleven weeks in 1992 with a fractured foot, had really given me a lot of time to think. The building trade was hard work, not that I was afraid of hard work. But during the winter months, the job could be hell. Plus I had (by some miracle) managed to come away from a major fall, relatively unscathed. But I certainly wouldn't want to try that a second time.

I remember one occasion we were tiling the roof of a hotel in Solihull. There had been a heavy downfall of snow during the previous evening and the temperature was freezing. I was trying to pick nails up out of a box and the nails were sticking to my fingers. It was the one and only time I have cried at work. I couldn't feel my fingers. I don't think I have ever felt that cold. Although it's fair to say, that the Long Mynd night hike came a close second.

I had always been so desperate to do something musically, but it never looked like anything would ever happen. J.B. Makin had actually contributed to my frustration inadvertently too; the roofing company had managed to get the contract to tile the roof of a huge extension that was being built onto the Columbia Hotel in London.

I was one of the workers sent to work on the roof. The fact that we were working on a hotel was quite handy, as this would also be our accommodation for the duration of the job. Fine by me, as it was a very nice hotel, and they served the most amazing full English breakfast.

To wind down, we used to have a few drinks in the hotel bar at night and one evening, there was this strange looking group of men, showing some American girls a piece of artwork. It looked like a vinyl record cover. I just put two and two together and thought that they must be a band.

The next night, we were having a meal in the hotel and at one of the tables sat two young guys dressed really garishly, 'It must be another band', I thought. One of them kept looking at my workmate, Giuseppe, who was a well-built Italian guy. Giuseppe was a really nice guy. He certainly wasn't the kind a guy that would start trouble. However, he did take offence to the stranger looking over at him constantly. Giuseppe said to me, "If that weirdo looks at me again, I'll knock his teeth out." Eventually the weird looking guys left and calmness was restored.

I said to the barman that night, "There seems to be a lot of strange looking people staying at the hotel. Are they musicians?" "Yes," he said, "the bands appearing on *Top of the Pops* usually stay here. I once met Simple Minds, they were really great guys."

The next day, I was having lunch in the hotel, when one of the musicians walked into the foyer, carrying four designer bags. I just remember feeling really jealous. Whoever these guys were, they appeared to be living the high life. This just fuelled my desire to work in music even more. I couldn't get these guys out of my head. It may sound strange, but I remember thinking, 'Why did I have to end up working on this hotel'. I wanted to know who they were and how this whole thing had happened to them. Was it fate that I ended up here? Some unknown force, trying to give me the drive I needed to persevere with my own music.

When I watched that week's *Top of the Pops*. It turned out that the artwork guys were The Inspiral

Carpets, they were performing 'This is how it Feels'. The guy my friend wanted to beat up was the lead singer of the duo Candy Flip. They were performing a dreadful cover version of The Beatles song, 'Strawberry Fields'.

I said to Giuseppe, "Imagine if you'd have blacked his eye, you could have pointed to the TV and said, 'Look mum, I did that'." We both chuckled.

The thing is though, that whole experience really did stay with me for a long time. To say I was envious would be a massive understatement.

When I finally had my leg plaster removed and went back to work, I had only been back for a week and then got laid off, due to a lack of work. Things were so slack, I was offered voluntary redundancy. They didn't need to ask twice.

********

I started to think about returning to education, and in 1992 enrolled myself on an Access into Higher Education course in humanities at Bilston Community College. The idea of this particular course was to give people access to university, without having to complete 'A' levels. You had to attain credits in the subjects of numeracy, history/literature, communications and education studies.

I met some great people on that course, who just like me, were serious music lovers. There was Lee Harris, who introduced me to the band Suede, whose debut album was brilliant. It was very reminiscent of early David Bowie.

Lee really knew his music. He looked cool too, with straight shoulder length hair, a look I'd often try to create, but my hair just wouldn't allow it.

Mine grew out rather than down. So it would always end up looking like a white afro, think Bob Marley, on the cover of the *Catch a Fire* album.

Then there was David Murphy, who was a huge Kinks and Beatles fan. I really looked up to Dave. He was naturally intelligent. He could talk to anyone about any subject and hold his own.

On our last day of term, we decided to stay in the class and play a game of hangman on the blackboard. Our theme was TV and film. I thought of a programme I just knew no one would guess, because it was too obscure. I began to draw my lines on the board:

_ _ _ / _ _ _ _ _ / _ _ / _ _ _ _ / _ _ _ _ _ _

Dave asked for the letter A

So I drew it in:

_ _ _ / _ _ _ _ _ / _ _ / _ _ _ _ / _ _ _ _ a _

Then he just came out with it ... "*The Sword of Tipu Sultan.*"

I was stunned! Dave is as sharp as a knife.

Even though I was making new friends at college, I was still spending most weekends with Lewi, Johno and Jacko. We used to start our drinking sessions in The Varisty pub in Wolverhampton, and then around 11pm, we'd make our way over the road to the Student Web nightclub, we loved this club because they played alternative music.

The owner of the club was this old man called Norman. He was openly gay and a very strange looking fellow to say the least. He was very short and had dark hair that looked like a toupee. He reminded me of a mini Lionel Blair.

He knew us quite well, because we were there every week. So he'd always have a chat, he would say "Have a nice time." Then he'd feel all our genitals as we walked past him. It happened so often it became the norm (pardon the pun) and we never used to bat an eyelid.

On one particular Friday evening, we were in the Varsity pub in Wolverhampton, when Johno produced some pills.

"Want to try some of these?" he asked.

"What are they?" I answered.

"Dexedrine, it's an amphetamine, it's like speed," he replied.

We all knew how popular speed had been within the Mod movement of the 60s. The pills back then were called Purple Hearts, which apparently were triangular in shape and blue in colour. The Dexedrine tablets were round and white.

I hadn't tried drugs before. It surprised me really, because Johno was always the quieter, most sensible one of the group, so for him to introduce drugs was quite a shock to me at the time. Anyway, suffice to say, we tried them ... and loved them.

Dexedrine is a form of amphetamine that stimulates the central nervous system. It basically speeds everything up. This is why it's almost impossible to sleep after taking them, because you usually find your heart continues to race, long after getting home from clubbing. It is however, great if you like to dance, because you don't feel fatigue.

The first time you try pills is quite weird, mainly because nothing happens for a while and when you haven't tried them before, you really

65

don't know what to expect. I remember asking Johno, "What's supposed to happen?" He said, "Just relax, you will know when it kicks in." About 20 minutes later this overwhelming sense of euphoria came over me and I couldn't stop talking. I was hyperactive.

I just remember thinking that it was the best feeling in the world. It got to the point where we HAD to have drugs on a Friday and Saturday night. Lewi would be really fucking miserable if we couldn't get any. I remember him saying to me, "I am never going to stop taking these pills." I felt exactly the same to be honest.

Now, they do say that wherever there's an up there's a down, and this is certainly the case with speed, because it makes sleep almost impossible. Most of the time I'd just lie in bed listening to music. Sometimes I wouldn't sleep a wink all night.

The next morning you would feel like shit, because you hadn't slept and then you'd start to come down. This was a really horrible feeling. It left you feeling exhausted and moody.

********

My Access course had gone well and I had obtained enough credits for a pass. However, I didn't get into university that year. I just thought that I might as well enrol on another one year course and try and get into university the following year. The big question was what to study next? I had wracked my brains desperately trying to think of something I really enjoyed doing.

Aside from music, I couldn't really think of anything that had really inspired me. Then I remembered ... *The Wizard of Oz*.

Although that performance seemed like a lifetime ago, I could still recall the feeling it gave me. I immediately picked up the new Bilston College prospectus and inside, there it was, listed in all its glory, the 'A' level Theatre and Film Studies courses.

There was another vivid memory burned into my brain from my time at J.B. Makin. One summer, we had been re-roofing a building at the Dudley campus, of the University of Wolverhampton. It was a scorching hot day and the work was torturous. I remember looking down from the roof and seeing masses of students sitting on the grass drinking cold beer. It was a depressing sight. If I was ever going to have a roofing accident, it's a wonder it didn't happen that day, as I felt like throwing myself off.

That's it, I just HAVE to get into university. I quickly enrolled on both the Theatre and Film Studies course and met fellow student Sue Hay. Sue was another highly intelligent person, who would become a real mentor to me over the years. We are still good friends to this day.

I loved theatre studies, because there was a good balance between the theory and practical work. I also enjoyed film studies, which obviously involved watching lots of films. We'd watch German Expressionist films like *The Cabinet of Doctor Caligari* and *Nosferatu,* and Italian Neorealist films such as *Bicycle Thieves.* The lecturer used to bring bags of sweets for the screenings. I think this was used as a bribe though, because he'd often play tennis in the afternoon, leaving us to view the films on our own.

I failed my theatre studies exam, but managed to pass my Film 'A' level. I reapplied to attend university on a theatre studies course, which was due to commence in September 1994.

********

During the summer of 1994, whilst shopping on a Saturday afternoon, I was approached by a complete stranger.

"Want to buy some drugs?" he asked.

"What you got?" I replied.

"I can get you anything you want."

I thought about it for a moment … "No, I am ok thanks."

"Ok, well anytime you need anything, let me know, I am always around town."

Now, this freaked me out be honest, I wondered why he had targeted me? I started to get paranoid, maybe I looked like a drug user.

About a month later, I was in town again, trying to find a new t shirt for my Saturday night out. I was walking down the main high street, when I saw the stranger again. I suddenly had this crazy idea. Imagine if I turned up at Lewi's house with a huge bag of pills. He'd be the happiest man in the world. I had this vision of me walking into his room and throwing a ton of pills onto his bed. I had to do it, so I ran to catch the guy up.

"Remember me?" I asked. "You said you could get drugs."

"Yeah man, what ya looking for?"

"Dexedrine pills."

"Sure, I can get you as many as you want man, how much you got?"

I told him I had forty quid. The pills usually cost £1 each and you'd take four at a time, so I was hoping to get 40 pills.

He told me to follow him, so I did. I had no idea where we were going, so thought it might be prudent to ask.

"Where are we going?"

"To a flat just outside town," was his response.

"Why you want so many pills?" he asked.

"To share with my mates," I replied.

"That's nice man, it's all about sharing. You seem like a nice guy, I tell you what, I will get you 50 pills for the £40 cause you seem like a good guy."

"That's great man! Are you sure?" I asked.

"Yeah man, no problem."

We eventually arrived at the flats right opposite the Molineux football stadium, on Waterloo Road. We walked up the first flight of stairs. Then he stopped.

"Right man, give us yer money, I need you to wait here, cause if my crew see your face at the door, that ain't gonna go down too well, you get me?"

"Yeah mate no worries."

I handed over my money and sat down on the stairs. It was at that precise moment I asked myself the question, 'What the fuck am I doing here?' I was all alone and anything could happen. At one point I looked at my watch. Fifteen minutes had passed and no sign of the drugs. I waited forty-five minutes. I knew at that point, that this wasn't going to end well.

I walked to the top of the stairs and travelled along the corridor, putting my ear close to all the doors, to see if I could hear the deal going down. Although, had I have heard anything, I have no idea what I'd have done. It was not like I was going to knock on the door was it. Can you imagine some dude answering the door with a machete or semi-automatic rifle and me saying, 'Excuse me, but I have been waiting for forty-five minutes now. Can

I please just have my drugs so I can get out of here?'

There was no sign of him, in fact, once I got to the end of the corridor, I reached a door to another staircase, I walked down the stairs and realised that this was another entrance to the building. I had been robbed. He must have taken my money, ran along the top floor, down the stairs and out the other end of the building. My heart sank. I had just blown my budget for the weekend.

That evening, I went round to Lewi's house. I told him that I wouldn't be able to go out, and proceeded to explain the story. He found it hilarious.

"What were you thinking?" he asked. "You could've been shot or anything."

"I know, I know, I wasn't really thinking. I kept having this vision of me throwing a boatload of pills onto your bed. He offered me 50 pills for 40 quid."

"Oh man, that's classic," was Lewi's response.

"Anyway, I'm skint now, so can't come out."

"Don't be daft. We'll all chip in to help you out."

So, each of my mates gave me ten pounds each and we went out.

From that moment on, I was always on the lookout for my drug dealer/con artist acquaintance. But I never saw him again. Lewi used to laugh and say, "Yo ay seeing him again Davo, he's fled the country wi ya money. He's probably living it up in Spain."

After using amphetamines for quite a while, I started to develop some serious side effects, none of which my friends ever experienced themselves. Firstly, for some reason, the high from speed never lasted as long for me, as it did for my mates. I used to get a three hour high then I'd start to come down. So, the night would still be young, when all of a sudden I would feel a tidal wave of depression come over me. I would often just leave my mates and go and find a corner of the club and sit on my own.

I started to smoke too, but only at weekends, this was also a symptom of the speed. It was either smoke or chew gum...usually at 100 miles per hour. I had chewed copious amounts of gum in the past, but I would get an unbelievable jaw ache the next day.

One particular evening, I had wondered off on my own at a club night called Red Balloon, which took place at Subway City in Birmingham. I can remember feeling really low. I have no idea why, but I had a sudden urge to put my cigarette out on my arm.

It didn't even seem to hurt that much. It is a weird thing to say, but it actually made me feel better. I have no idea why, no rational explanation at all.

It got to the point where I was constantly pressing lit cigarettes against my arm.

On another occasion in Red Balloon I had started to come down off drugs and began to burn my arm again. I didn't realise that a girl was watching me. I caught her eye and she seemed to leave really quickly. I got a bad feeling, so I moved onto the dance floor, when about two minutes later all these security guys appeared with torches. Searching the area where I had been sitting. They were obviously looking for me.

Getting myself banned from Red Balloon would have been a disaster. We loved that club. The club had multiple rooms, playing a wide variety of great music. We'd spend the majority of the night in the back room, which played all the classic mod tunes.

I would request some of my favourite songs, such as 'The Champ' by The Mowhawks, 'She's Got Everything' by The Kinks, 'Gimme Some Lovin' by Spencer Davis Group and 'Making Time' by The Creation.

I knew absolutely nothing about self-harming. It was a subject that was very rarely publicised. The only other person I'd heard about was Richey Edwards from the band Manic Street Preachers.

In 1991 after a show at Norwich Arts Centre, Richey got into an argument with the journalist Steve Lamacq. Steve was questioning the authenticity of the band, so Richey proceeded to carve the words '4 real' into his arm using a razor blade.

I'd first seen the Manic Street Preachers on the TV show *Top of the Pops* in 1992, performing the single 'You Love Us'. The lead singer James' posturing, wearing nothing but white skinny jeans and the words 'You Love Us' scrawled across his bare chest in red lipstick, just fascinated me. Not because there was anything shocking about it. My interest came from the fact that it was miles away from what was going on musically during the early 1990s.

This was the 'baggy' era, with bands such as Happy Mondays and Stone Roses.

Everything had to be a 'loose fit'. Manic Street Preachers flew in the face of the baggy ethic.

Released in 1992, *Generation Terrorists*, their aptly named debut was purchased on release date from Our Price records in Dudley, West Midlands and came as a double album in a gatefold sleeve.

Richey's role within the band was lyricist and rhythm guitarist. It was common knowledge that Richey wasn't a great musician. This never really bothered me though, mainly because his lyrics were so good. Oh...and he was cool too. He had such an amazing presence on and off the stage.

My brother and I were watching them on their *Gold Against the Soul* tour at Wolverhampton Civic Hall in 1993, when after the encore Richey left his leather jacket on the mike stand. As the audience started to clear, I can remember thinking that I could so easily grab it off the stage, even the security had started to disperse.

"Ian, hang on, I am going to grab Richey's jacket."

"You can't take his jacket!"

"Why not?"

"Because it's not your jacket."

As soon as my brother uttered those words, the moment had gone. There was no way I could take it now. Plus, I had never been a thief and this would in fact be theft.

Richey had co-written album lyrics with bass player Nicky Wire, but on their third album, *The Holy Bible*, the majority of the lyrics were penned by Richey.

*The Holy Bible* is widely thought of as one of the darkest albums in history. It deals with a wide variety of subject matter, including the holocaust and anorexia.

Richey was obviously a very sensitive and troubled soul.

In 1995 ahead of a US promotional tour, he disappeared and was never seen again.

## University of Wolverhampton and cock-blocking Simon Le Bon

I remember the first day of term quite vividly, because the night before I had watched an episode of Channel 4's television soap opera, *Brookside*, and in my introductory lecture I was certain that I had seen one of its actors sitting opposite me. After the lecture I approached him.

"Were you in *Brookside* last night?"

"Yes."

"Impressive. How did you get on *Brookside*? Can you get me on?"

I got the impression that Owen was thinking, 'Wow wow slow down! 'Now, considering that this was a theatre studies course, meeting someone who had been on TV was a big deal.

His name was Owen Lewis and he hailed from Shrewsbury in Shropshire.

From that moment on we became inseparable, even though there was an age difference; Owen was 34 and I was 24. We got along famously. I was soon to find out that Owen was also a music lover, although his musical roots stemmed from traditional folk music. He actually played an instrument too. His choice of instrument is the harmonica.

Prior to university, he had been a regional radio DJ, as well as appearing in various television programmes in a featured role, or as an extra.

As well as meeting Owen, I got to meet the very wise Angela Hunt. Angie hailed from Bristol and was my go to person for advice. She is such a good listener and we became really close. Years later at a university reunion, she would help me steal a University of Wolverhampton sign from a door at the Dudley campus. Come to think of it, we stole a load of plants too.

Basically, the Dudley campus was closing down, much to our dismay and so during the reunion, Owen made a rebel rousing speech. 'Save the campus etc'. Eventually the night descended into total chaos. Not because of Owen's speech I might add! A group of troublemakers had been ejected from the building. They tried to get back in, but security stopped them, so they decided to smash some of the student union windows.

At the end of the night, Owen, Angie, Nick Fawdry and myself decided to take various bits of memorabilia, before they finally tore the place down...to build flats I believe.

As well as the new faces, Dudley campus was home to some familiar faces too. My college pal, Dave Murphy was there, although by the time I started, he had already been there a year.

Dave almost got into trouble for sneaking me into one of his poetry lectures. All was well, until the lecturer started to read a poem aloud containing the line 'the helmeted pump'. The lecturer really accentuated the words and I couldn't stop sniggering. This set Dave off too. Luckily, I didn't get Dave into trouble, but I thought it best not to infiltrate any more of his lectures.

There was also my college theatre studies friend, Sue Hay. She had obtained a degree in Arts and English Literature before she'd even started at Wolverhampton. She'd completed it through the Open University. Sue would be celebrating her 48th birthday in the November of our first term. To be honest, it was great to have that level of maturity on the theatre studies course, because a lot of the younger students hadn't yet grasped the importance of time keeping, especially during rehearsals. Sue wouldn't take any crap and would always put the late-comers in their place.

I had bought myself a second hand blue Pk125 Vespa motor scooter, to get myself to and from university. Lewi was always adamant that we had to look the part, even on our scooters, so encouraged me to buy an open faced helmet. My look would be finished off with a cream mac and paisley cravat.

The three years I spent at university were brilliant. It really did confirm my love of acting. During the course we studied some of the world's leading theatre practitioners, such as Stanislavski, Brecht and Artuad. We would then stage plays, utilising each practitioner's style of acting and production.

Yet again, the course had a good balance between the practical and theory. For one of our plays, Steven Berkoff's *Agamemnon* I even got to incorporate some of my martial arts.

1994 was the year that Oasis released *Definitely Maybe* and Blur released *Parklife*. These two albums pretty much dominated the student union bar. Although I was never an Oasis fan, I couldn't escape the fact that they pretty much created the sound track to my entire time at university. There was however a glimmer of light, because we also had Pulp's *His 'n' Hers* album and a year later, their classic, *Different Class*.

1994 was also the year that I proposed to Jayne. It was however, to be a very long engagement.

********

By the latter part of 1996, my weekend drug taking was getting totally out of control. I was still living with my parents in Moxley and to help pay my way had taken a weekend job at Morrisons supermarket, on the wines and spirits department.

I'd take speed on a Friday evening and have to work on Saturday morning, then take speed Saturday night and have to work on Sunday morning. The only way I could get through my shifts was to start taking the drug at work. I never got caught doing this. However, I did start to wonder whether my boss might be getting suspicious, because I never wanted to take my break. I don't think she had ever seen anyone work so fast.

One Sunday, Jayne and I were having lunch at my parents, my t shirt sleeve must have moved up my arm just enough for Jayne to catch a glimpse of the marks on my arm. She grabbed my wrist and pulled my sleeve up. I will never forget the look on her face. There were around ten burn marks on my arm.

I could never eloquently explain my feelings to Jayne about what had been going on. But I did promise that I wouldn't do it again.

At that time, I could never imagine clubbing without drugs. They had been such a big part of the whole experience. I just thought that quitting would be like trying to climb a mountain.

Little did I know, that one major incident was about to make giving up drugs easier than I could ever have imagined.

By early 1997, Johno was no longer able to supply Dexedrine. From what I remember, the authorities began to realise that the drug was being abused on a major level. By that, I mean people were faking attention deficit hyperactive disorder and maybe even narcolepsy, just so they could be prescribed Dexedrine, which they'd then

77

sell on.

The pharmaceutical companies started to produce Dexedrine in liquid form. This was a nightmare for drug users, because you couldn't just put this in your pocket on the way to a club.

We did manage to obtain the liquid on a few occasions and I had what I thought was an ingenious idea. I turned up at Lewi's house with a tic-tac box. The idea would be to pour the liquid inside, then seal the lid with sellotape.

I emptied the sweets, then Lewi began to pour the liquid inside the little plastic sweet container. We never realised that there was a tiny pin hole in the bottom of the box and the liquid started squirting out. Lewi called out "Fuck! fuck! It's all coming out." He held his mouth under the hole to catch the remainder of the liquid.

Dexedrine in liquid form really was a non-starter for us, so we then started to score your regular run-of-the-mill amphetamine. I liked the idea of Dexedrine because it was a prescribed drug. The thing with powder form amphetamine is you never know what the drug is being cut with and believe me, dealers ALWAYS cut the drug. One wrap of speed to a drug dealer can become two, by just adding something like flour, or maybe a substance much worse, like Vim scouring powder!

Around the middle of 1997, my parents had gone away for the week. It was a Wednesday evening, when I got a call from Lewi saying he had managed to track down a new dealer. So we got on our scooters and rode over to the dealer's house.

We had a feeling he was new to the game, because when we got back to my house, we emptied the drugs onto my kitchen table, and it was like a white amphetamine mountain. We couldn't believe we'd been given such a large amount for £40.

The idea was to leave the drugs at mine, because it was safer, as my parents were away. As it turned out, this proved to be a bad idea. We weren't due to be going to a club until Friday night, but I ingested the drug on Wednesday, Thursday and Friday night.

Now, one of the other symptoms of amphetamine abuse is suppression of appetite and I have no recollection of eating anything on any of those three days.

On the Friday night, we rode our scooters to Moseley in Birmingham. A friend of ours was DJing a night at Moselcy Dancehall. We didn't sleep that night and rode back to Wolverhampton on Saturday morning. The idea was to go straight into town to buy some clothes, and then go for a coffee.

We were in TJ Hughes looking at clothes, when all of a sudden I felt really weird. I told Lewi that I needed to go outside and then I collapsed. I had never had a feeling like that before or since, it was like every single nerve ending in my fingers was vibrating at an incredible rate. I didn't know what was going on. Lewi looked terrified.

I called out to him, "Call me an ambulance."

"I ain't calling an ambulance!"

"You've got to, I think I'm dying."

It was such an out-of-body experience. It was a busy Saturday afternoon and yet I don't recall seeing any other people, just Lewi. It was like we were the only two people left after the apocalypse.

"I'll get you some food, you'll feel better. I can't call an ambulance because that's going to land us in a world of shit."

"I can't feel my fingers!"

79

"Come on, I need to get you off the floor."

He picked me up and literally walked me through the town holding onto my arm to support me. I was getting worse.

"You'll be ok I'll get you some food."

Lewi led me into a pub in the centre of town and bought me a glass of Coke and a Mars bar.

"Wait here, I am going to call a taxi."

The taxi dropped us back to his parents' house and he put me to bed and made me beans on toast.

Radiohead's *Ok Computer* had recently been released and he left it on whilst he was cooking my beans. Now I love Radiohead, but the song that plays in my mind whenever I recall this moment, is 'No Surprises'. That song will forever be associated with that incident. Yes indeed, music soundtracks both the happiest and saddest days of our lives.

Lewi's theory was that I was suffering from sleep deprivation and malnutrition. I did start to feel a little better as soon as I'd finished the food.

I fell asleep on his bed and when I woke up I said, "That's it man, I'm done, I can't do speed anymore." The whole experience had really scared me. And that was that. I never took speed ever again. As soon as the drug stopped, the self-harming stopped.

Lewi carried on taking speed for some time after I had stopped and although my nights out were a little strange without drugs, I couldn't help but think that the incident had been a warning. I had managed to tell the tale this time, but I may not be so lucky next time.

I was still partial to the odd spliff. Owen was really into cannabis too, so we'd often get together and have a smoke and put the world to rights.

Owen used to compere some of the entertainment events at university. He was brilliant at it. On one occasion, he was on stage, when this girl handed him an address for an after show house party. The house was in Wolverhampton, but we didn't get there until 3am. Little did we know that the actual person who'd invited us had left the party hours ago.

We knocked on the door, still buzzing and well up for a party. We had beers in hand and a huge amount of cannabis.

This sheepish guy answered the door and told us the party was over.

Owen said, "But we've bought all these beers."

The guy said, "Oh, well you can come in if you like, but nearly everyone else has left."

The remainder of the people were gathered in one of the main bedrooms. There were two lads and three girls. It was an awkward moment, but Owen broke the ice with "Who'd like a joint then?" At that moment, the girls seemed to bounce back to life.

There was one guy however, who really didn't appreciate our intrusion. He was the spitting image of Simon Le Bon from the band Duran Duran and he didn't show any interest in us whatsoever, no hello or anything. In fact, his first words were, "You know guys we were really winding the party down now." One of the girl's replied, "Chill out, I want to have a joint."

Those were the only words Owen needed to hear and he quickly proceeded to take out his drug paraphernalia.

"Can I use the toilet please?" I asked.

"Yeah, I'll show you where it is," replied the chap that had answered the door.

Once we were outside the room, I asked, "What's wrong with Simon Le Bon?"

"Who?"

"Old grumpy bum sitting on the bed," I replied.

"Oh, I think he felt he was almost getting close with one of the girls, but I guess he is worried you may have ruined his chance now."

"We'll just have a quick smoke and leave if you like?"

"No rush, it's fine."

When I got back to the room, the cannabis production line was now fully functional and Owen was producing joints at an unbelievable rate.

I don't think I have ever seen anyone roll a joint like Owen. It is a sight to behold. Me on the other hand, I am useless. Mine always used to fall apart and I would often rely on someone else to salvage the situation, with a quick repair job.

One joint turned into two, then into three. Simon Le Bon suddenly pipes up, "I am off to bed now." He lingered, waiting for a response. No response came. So he just left the room.

We left the party about two hours later and couldn't stop laughing at how we had cock-blocked poor old Simon Le Bon. Walking along the streets of Wolverhampton at 5am, I looked at Owen and started singing, "Bop bop bop, bop bop bop bop bop, this is planet earth."

Owen pointed at me with both hands and called out, "You're looking at planet earth."

********

I had decided to start taking classical piano lessons and found a teacher in Wolverhampton, called Sophia Humphreys, who originally came from Greece. In her youth, she had been a well-respected pianist and had even performed piano recitals on Greek radio.

This fuelled my desire to start a university musical side project, mainly because our great hall had a full sized grand piano and no one ever used it, which I thought was a total waste. The project consisted of Owen on harmonica and vocals, Gemma Crammond on flute, Rich Goodhall on bass and myself on piano.

Rich was to become another very close friend. He majored in English, but picked up a few drama modules during his first semester. The first time I met him was in a drama workshop, where we were instructed to walk around the room and make eye contact with each other, without speaking (a classic acting exercise). Anyway, our eyes met and we just both burst helplessly into laughter, much to the lecturer's dismay.

Later that week he asked me if I fancied lunch at his house, as it was close to the campus. I accepted and we made our way onto the main road where all the cars were parked that couldn't find space on the university car park.

Amongst the cars was a red Porsche. I said jokingly, "I bet that's yours isn't it?" He laughed and said, "Yes." It was indeed Rich's car.

Rich is one of those dependable people that would literally drop everything to help someone out. He's a genuinely nice guy. However, there is a fly in the ointment. He supports my football team's main rival, West Bromwich Albion.

Rich is a rocker at heart, his favourite band is Led Zeppelin.

Our university band never had a proper name, but we often referred to ourselves as the 'Doctors of Semiotics'. Not in any way pretentious.

We used to rehearse in the main hall at university, but there was a jobsworth caretaker who kept trying to boot us out, for some reason he just didn't want us in there, even though we were doing something constructive.

I remember the first time he showed up. To be fair to him, he did wait at the back of the hall until we had finished our song, before he piped up:

"Have you had permission to be in here?"

"No," replied Owen.

"Well you shouldn't be in here."

"We aren't doing any harm, just rehearsing for an hour." I said.

"And you shouldn't be on that piano without permission."

These words were like a red rag to a bull and Owen came out with the most eloquent of outbursts ... "This is our university, we are here to learn, push ourselves, to be creative. Why is us being in here such a huge problem for you, are you simply on a power trip? There are much worse things we could be doing with our time you know. We'll get permission next time, now can you just stop wasting our valuable time please and leave."

The caretaker mumbled under his breath, then left the hall, leaving the doors wide open. Then, like a gazelle, Owen leapt off the stage and started running towards the back of the hall. I thought, fuck, Owen's going to attack the caretaker! But upon reaching the back of the hall, Owen just slammed all the doors shut and returned to the stage.

I can't believe how much energy I had back then. There were so many projects going on all at once. During our second year of university, Sue, Owen and me even started a theatre company called MOLD, the name of which came from Owen's and my initials.

Sue Hay was company director and suggested

we perform *The Dumb Waiter* by Harold Pinter, because it was a two-hander, which meant Sue could direct it and Owen and me could act in it. Then we had another student, Claire Hand as stage manager. Sue's husband Bob even made a fully functioning dumb waiter out of wood.

We took the play to various venues, including Shrewsbury Boathouse, The Newhampton Inn and the Arena Theatre, Wolverhampton. We'd even managed to get some good press to advertise the show too.

I almost lost teeth during the curtain call at Shrewsbury, when Owen took the bow with his metal gun still in hand. He raised his arms and smacked me right in the mouth.

My university experience wouldn't have been half as enjoyable without Owen, Sue and Claire (also a big Morrissey fan). We were like glue, permanently stuck together, especially Owen and me. It was such a good laugh. I also got to know his wife and beautiful daughter, Lottie. Years later Owen would shock me right to the core, by announcing to me that he was gay. Of course, it didn't affect our relationship. I love Owen to bits. He is like a brother, and one of only a handful of people, whose presence makes living this life just that little bit easier.

We all graduated in 1997 and I managed to leave university with a 2:1 in Theatre and History, and at that point the only thing I could see myself doing, was acting. I had managed to get myself an equity card and set about starting working life as a jobbing actor.

## An Actor's Life for Me

Sue Hay had written our dissertation play. It was called *One of the Boys* and was about the 1940s world light heavyweight boxing champion, Freddie Mills, who was found shot dead in his car at the back of the nightclub he owned in July 1965. Although the coroner's verdict was suicide, there was always a big question mark over his death with the possibility that it could have been a gang land killing.

After our graduation ceremony, we decided to take the play to the 1997 Edinburgh Fringe Festival, which is the largest arts festival in the world and features everything from theatre and comedy to music and dance. It was a great experience and so began my love affair with the Edinburgh Fringe.

I returned the following year starring in an adaptation of *Wuthering Heights*, which was written and directed by Negative Equity Theatre Company, which was a company specialising in physical theatre and run by husband and wife, Pete Machen and Rebekah Fortune. They had also performed in Edinburgh the previous year, with their critically acclaimed show *Killing Larry*.

I wrote and recorded the music for *Wuthering Heights*. I recorded it in my house, using keyboards and a Tascam four track tape recorder. It was the first time I had attempted to score a play and the company was really happy with the results.

In 1999, I made my third consecutive appearance at the Edinburgh Fringe. Sue Hay had suggested the idea of doing a one man show about the British Monarchy.

Sue wrote and directed the entire one hour show and called it *A Load of Old Monarchs.* The show would portray 60 monarchs in sixty minutes. As well as numerous costume changes, the play contained songs utilising a variety of instruments, including guitar, accordion and piano, which I played live.

You are never guaranteed good audience figures at the fringe, unless your show has a star, or there is already a buzz about the show, or you are a successful comedian of course. So you have to rely heavily on getting good press reviews to help generate public interest.

We had booked Bedlam Theatre for the show, which was on the corner of Bristow Place, in central Edinburgh. The theatre is actually housed in an old church and has a terrific atmosphere. On the opening day of the show, we had only sold one ticket. The theatre had a policy whereby if there were less than five people present, you had the option to cancel. Sue came backstage and informed me of the situation.

"There is only one man in the audience, what do you want to do?"

"Does he still want to watch it?" I asked.

"I'll go and ask."

A couple of minutes later she came back.

"Yes, he wants to watch it."

"Ok, I'll do it."

So I ended up performing our one-man show to one person.

A few days later we got press in to review it and received a four star review.

The Scotsman wrote:
*'A jolly olde spoof about the kings and queens*

*of England, this effervescent romp through history from Alfred the Great to the present is designed for those who don't mind turning up sober for a goofy cabaret act on a book-learned topic in the middle of the afternoon. At this particular performance there were only five of us, but Martin Davies found our funny bone anyway ...Davies effortlessly clowns through any weak spots and hits the highs right in the solar plexus.'*

Now, what I love most about the Edinburgh Fringe is the overall atmosphere of the festival and camaraderie of the performers. Part of the whole experience involves trying to sell your show, by giving out fliers or actually performing on the Royal Mile. This is a thoroughfare that forms part of the old town of Edinburgh and gets its name as it is exactly one Scots mile long. The festival office is also based on the Royal Mile.

During this particular year, new rules were being introduced, whereby street performers were not being allowed to perform on the Royal Mile, unless they had public liability insurance and a security firm was introduced to police the streets.

We had no idea this was going on when we arrived, so there I was, along with everyone else, stepping onto the Royal Mile, ready to promote the show with my accordion strapped over my shoulder, when I got stopped by security.

"Sorry, you can't play that along here."

"You are destroying this festival mate." I replied.

I just sat down on the kerb, thinking that this whole situation was complete bullshit.

To be honest, I thought this would kill the spirit of the festival. It really did wind me up, this, coupled with the fact that the comedy really appeared to be dominating the festival during this particular year too.

I was still sitting on the kerb, when this man approached me. As soon as I saw his face, I thought he looked familiar, but I just couldn't put a name to the face. He had a distinctive moustache and beard, very reminiscent of the Frans Hals portrait, 'The Laughing Cavalier'.

"Have you been told to stop playing?"

"Yes," I replied.

"Well this afternoon at 1pm, I am holding a protest outside the festival office. I want to say 'NO' to the new rules. I'm Jim Rose, from the Jim Rose Circus and lots of press are going to cover the protest. Do you want to take part?"

"Definitely," I replied.

Then he left, continuing his mission to recruit more performers.

'Ah Jim Rose', I thought.

I had seen his circus on television. His show had freaky performers, who did things like swallow swords and push nails through their tongues etc.

I turned up at 12:30pm and a large amount of performers had already started to gather. I had put my *A Load of Old Monarchs* t shirt on, hoping there might be a press photo that makes it into the paper. This would be a great advert for our show.

The t shirt decision turned out to be a good call.

All the performers stood behind Jim as he announced to the press:

"We are saying 'No' to the new rules. As a protest, I am going to place an apple in someone's mouth, and then with my chainsaw, I am going to cut the word no into it."

Now at that very moment, I must have had what can only be described as a 'jumping the roofs flashback' because I grabbed Jim's arm and said, "I want the apple." Then Jim exclaimed, "And this gentleman will have the apple." The crowd cheered.

I didn't feel nervous to be honest, well, not until Jim put the apple in my mouth, then whispered in my ear, "Whatever you do, don't fucking move!" At that point I started to sweat. Then he started the chainsaw, and as he moved it within two inches of my face, I was crapping myself.

The chainsaw was spitting fuel onto my face, so I closed my eyes. There was a cheer, which I assumed meant he must have finished. I breathed a HUGE sigh of relief. I couldn't believe what I had just done. It certainly wasn't a wise thing to do.

I don't think my director, Sue, was too happy either.

The upside was ... it made all the papers. In fact it made the front page of most of them. And in the photos, there it was in all its glory, my *A Load of Old Monarchs* t shirt. It was an advertising dream, even if I did nearly have to lose part of my face to get it.

After returning from Edinburgh, I auditioned and got the part of Spike in a musical called *Go and Play Further*...the sequel to the hugely successful *Go and Play up Your Own End*, which had completed a sell-out run at Solihull Arts Complex and then went on to do the same at the Birmingham Hippodrome. The script was written by Malcolm Stent and based on his book of the same name, it was about his childhood growing up in Birmingham. Malcolm is a bit of a Brummie legend and is mainly known for his comedy and music. Malcolm had been a regular at The Boggery which was a folk club started by Jasper Carrot in the late 60s.

I was now starting to get regular work, which included everything from local radio voice-overs to school tours. One of the most memorable schools tours was a production of *Macbeth*, in which I was playing the part of Macbeth.

My employer was Katch 22 productions, who coincidentally were the company that had put on *Go and Play up Your Own End*. It was run by another husband and wife, Steve Kray and Ash O'Reailly.

Steve is a great actor and director, and had managed to put together a really nice abridged version of Shakespeare's classic tragedy.

We turned up at one school and I noticed that the ceiling of the hall was covered in helium balloons. I never thought anything else about it.

During Act2, scene 1 of *Macbeth* you have the famous 'dagger scene' Where Macbeth imagines a dagger floating in front of him, leading him toward, the king, Duncan, who he is about to kill. This is always a difficult scene to perform, because the audience needs to really believe that Macbeth can actually see a dagger. It can prove even more difficult for children to grasp the actual concept.

My belief was that the only way you were going to get the children to believe the scene, was by acting it convincingly. Couple this with the right atmosphere on stage and it should work.

The lights would come down, then a little dry ice was pumped onto the stage and the scene was set.

I began the famous soliloquy:

*Is this a dagger which I see before me,*
*The handle toward my hand?*
*Come, let me clutch thee.*

91

*I have thee not, and yet I see thee still.*
*Art thou not, fatal vision, sensible*
*To feeling as to sight? or art thou but*
*A dagger of the mind, a false creation...*

All of a sudden, I heard a few sniggers from the audience. This threw me a little, because no one had ever laughed during this scene before. It gradually got louder. It actually felt like half the audience were laughing out loud.

Then all became clear. Out of the corner of my eye, I could see a balloon gradually descending.

Shakespeare can be difficult to remember at the best of times, what with it being so wordy. This certainly wasn't helping. The balloon landed on the throne, then moved its way across the front of the stage. At that moment, I considered stepping on it, but that was only going to bring me out of the scene and probably make them laugh even more.

I remember thinking, 'So much for the audiences' suspension of disbelief'.

The balloon eventually dropped off the front of the stage and the kids finally settled down. The other actors and stage hands hadn't seen what was going on, so they were back stage having a panic, wondering what on earth was happening. They all had a good laugh about it later though.

********

The year 2000 turned out to be a crazy year. During January I had started rehearsals for a play, which was going to be performed on the London Fringe at the Finborough Theatre, Earl's Court. The play was a comedy called *Christmas in July* and was about a man called John, played by myself, who, although in a gay relationship is unsure of his sexuality. He gets his former flat-mate pregnant after an office party. The tension eventually reaches boiling point, due to the entire seemingly hopeless situation of this bizarre ménage a trois.

I was rehearsing the play during the day and trying to help Jayne with wedding plans during the evening. But it's fair to say that Jayne pretty much organised the wedding single-handedly.

Our wedding was due to take place at Dunstall Racecourse, Wolverhampton on Saturday 26th August.

*Christmas in July* was a joy to be part of, and was critically well received.

The Wandsworth Times wrote:
*'With acrid lines from Sam like: 'trust me to end up with a closet straight!" and the bitter-sweet musical soliloquies from Sarah, along with John's earnestness, the play deserves praise and is well worth a trip. I hope you make that trip. This young company, based in Birmingham deserves to be seen.'*

After *Christmas in July*, I went straight into rehearsals for a stage adaptation of Robert Louis Stevenson's *Treasure Island*. Then I was cast in another musical called *Balfour*. Again, this was to be produced by Katch 22 productions. The main star of the show was local BBC Radio WM legend, Malcolm Boydon, who was one of the nicest people I have ever met and a great sport too; I had this idea that I pitched to him at a rehearsal one day. I said, "Malcolm, if we give you a new word or phrase every day, can you try and slip it into your radio show?" Well Malcolm thought it was a great idea. The first words I gave him were 'trench foot'.

I don't think any of the cast members expected Malcolm to make an entire feature of it on his radio show, but that's exactly what he did.

He asked his audience live on air, "Does anyone know anything about trench foot? If so, can you please phone the show, I'd love to hear from you."

The amount of calls he got from these lovely old dears was amazing. One phoned up and said, "That trench foot is supposed to be horrible, however, if you do get it, I can recommend Germolene antiseptic cream, that will clear it up."

It was hilarious. We even got him to say 'Griffin's Bridge' on air...the name given to a certain private part of the body. Luckily this wasn't a common phrase and only known by a small circle of friends or else Malcolm would have been fired on the spot.

Our wedding day was fantastic and quite eventful. Jayne looked gorgeous in her dress, which had been hand made by her sister, Dawn.

I got roped into singing Pulp's 'Common People' during the evening. We had Jacko caught by my mother-in-law trying to throw Lewi's boxer shorts out of a bedroom window and wedding guests stripping off, whilst running around the race track like horses.

Malcolm Boydon even called my wife up live on air, during the morning of our wedding day. She was at her sister-in-law's salon, having her hair done. The call was so funny, because the salon sounded so chaotic. I am not sure if the wedding party had started drinking early, but all you could hear in the background was a cacophony of really loud laughter and the humming of hairdryers.

This wasn't the first time I'd sang 'Common People'. It was becoming a bit of a party piece. The first time I'd attempted the song, was at a student union karaoke night. I thought it might be funny to try and impersonate Pulp's singer Jarvis Cocker, whilst singing the song, however, someone in the crowd took offence to this and threw an empty pint glass at me, missing my face by inches.

The stewards were on to him like a swarm of bees and he was thrown out. It didn't really phase me at all. The show must go on and all that. I got to the end of the song and got a standing ovation.

There was no honeymoon immediately after the wedding, because the following day, I was straight back into rehearsals for *Balfour*.

## Put the Needle Down and Fly

Although busy with my acting, I was still trying to make time for music and it was a night at Ronnie Scott's Birmingham in 1999 that really changed everything for me musically. I can't remember why this actually happened, but I had left Twister and started playing keyboards again in a band called, Lasso the moon, which was a four piece from Walsall. The lead singer/songwriter was named Nigel Brookes, who had also been a student at the University of Wolverhampton. In fact, he had dated one of my classmates.

Nigel was a good songwriter and managed to pen some really decent songs.

As a band we drew influences from both the folk and jazz world and I had ditched the synthesizers, in favour of a Fender Rhodes piano and Hammond organ, which Nigel had kindly purchased for me.

We had been booked to headline an acoustic night at Ronnie Scott's bar in Birmingham. In the audience that night were two members of the now defunct cult 80s band, Felt.

Between 1982 and 1989, Felt had released ten studio albums. The band had started out on the Cherry Red label and then later signed to Alan Magee's Creation Records, the label that would eventually sign Oasis.

Marco Thomas had played on five of the Felt albums. He'd played bass on four of them and guitar on a fifth. Gary Ainge had played drums on all ten. After Felt disbanded, Gary and Marco had formed the instrumental band Fly.

The original fly line up had Martin Duffy on

keyboards, but Martin joined Primal Scream and I think the band found it hard to get a fully committed keyboard player after that. So, they had been on the lookout and decided to attend the Ronnie Scott's gig out of curiosity, as Gary knew our lead singer.

After the gig, Marco and Gary asked me if I would help them out on keyboards. To be honest, I hadn't heard of Felt, but when I listened to Fly's debut *Motorway* EP, I was blown away. The EP came out on 4M records in 1998 and the band had got a few positive articles in music papers, such as the NME. The EP contained the following tracks:

1. Motorway
2. Flyover
3. Street Signs

The music was right up my street, because it was heavily keyboard based, I also loved the fact that Marco played the bass guitar like a lead instrument. The bass was as big a feature of Fly's sound as say Peter Hook's was to New Order's or Mick Karn's to Japan's.

After rehearsing with Fly and writing new material, we recorded a demo CD with my good friend Johno from Twister, who owned a portable Yamaha digital studio. Johno was really getting into music production and produced a great demo recording for us.

Gary sent our demo to Louis Calvo, the owner of the independent record label, Elefant Records, who are based in Madrid. Louis had been a huge Felt fan and used to fly over to the UK to see them in the 80s. Gary thought this could be our way into the label. So we sent them our demo before anyone else.

97

Louis got back to us really quickly, stating that he really liked the demo and was more than willing to pay for us to record an album.

This was a dream come true.

It was a really creative period for me. Knowing we were going to record an album, well that really fuelled my creativity. I would spend hours at home, working on new material for the band. We didn't have that many finished songs, so we had to work hard to make sure we could at least deliver a ten track album.

We did eventually end up with ten tracks and all of them were titled by Felt's enigmatic front man, Lawrence. He also came up with the album title, *Put the Needle Down and Fly*.

The titles were:
Multiplex, Skislope, Motorway, Chalet, Flightpath, Scandinavia, Flyover, Liberation Lambourghini and Situation.

We began the recording session in February 2000 and I had to work the sessions around the *Christmas in July* show. The album was recorded by Jon Cotton at Artisan Studios, Birmingham and was produced by ourselves.

One of the main reasons for using Artisan Studios was that it had a fantastic collection of classic synthesizers, including the amazing Prophet 5 analogue synthesizer, which we utilised to great effect. The Prophet 5 has a great reputation, and throughout the years has been used by the likes of Gary Numan, Pink Floyd, Japan and New Order. They are quite hard to get hold of now and if you can find one, it will more than likely set you back in excess of £4000.

The album also featured keyboard contributions by John Holmes, who was an amazing session player and Primal Scream's Martin Duffy.

Elefant Records had put a lot of trust in us, because they were paying for recording time before we'd even signed a contract. The final contract wasn't signed until 2002.

The record label were a bit naughty, because their recording contract stipulated that we had to also sign a publishing deal with Elefant's publishing label, Elefant Publishing.

We would much rather have signed with a separate publishing company, however, in the end we just decided to go along with the deal, as there were no other offers on the table.

There would be a lengthy delay before the release, artwork had to be approved and final contracts needed to be drawn up.

Because our record label was based in Spain, everything seemed to take an age to complete. Their English wasn't great and our Spanish was even worse.

*Put the Needle Down and Fly* was eventually released on CD and limited edition vinyl early 2002.

Reviews were quite favourable. The NME wrote:
*'It takes three former members of 80s legends Felt, to revisit the kind of retro-futurism where jet travel and autobahns were the stuff of wild possibility. With titles helpfully provided by their former Felt leader, the eternally enigmatic Lawrence, 'Put the Needle Down and Fly' is chrome-silver Eurotronica, evoking household robots, Kraftwerk and synthesizers the size of a family car...when they hit their stride through the*

*neon lights, Fly sound as much now as then.'*

Record collector wrote:

*'Never quite as obscure as they appear, Fly excel on compositions such as 'Motorway', a commercial slice of New Order heavy-style pop with some nifty hi-hat work. Tracks like 'Chalet' and 'Scandinavia' may tread the same path as other songs here, but what's so interesting about this record is that it evokes so many images. 'Flyover' is a blessed out paean to endless autobahns. In sounding out of time, Fly sound like the future.'*

My only regret is that we never played a single live show. We often talked about it, but never arranged any gigs, so I suppose you could say that we were a studio band really.

Meeting Gary and Marco had a big impact on my life and really broadened my listening habits. Gary introduced me to the 1970s German Krautrock movement. With bands like Neu! , Can, Cosmic Jokers, Harmonia and Tangerine Dream and I grew to love them all.

I would see a lot more of Marco, as he lived in the Midlands, whereas Gary, although a fellow Midlander, now lived in London and only occasionally travelled up to the Midlands, to see family or for the occasional Fly rehearsal.

Marco's tastes range from classical right through to Jazz. He loves Bach, Pat Metheny, XTC and Genesis. In fact it was Marco that really got me into Peter Gabriel. I think the first song he ever played me was 'Here Comes the Flood', which was off Gabriel's debut album. I became hooked after that and bought his entire back catalogue.

If someone had told me that in five years' time,

I would be getting to meet him, I would have laughed, but in May 2007 that's exactly what happened.

Fly never officially split up. It was more of a case of it being put on the back burner. The music was such an acquired taste, that I was always very realistic about what we could achieve. I knew *Put the Needle Down and Fly* was never going to set the world alight and go on to sell a million copies. I did however, hope that we'd make a second album, but we never did.

Marco and I would still get together on a regular basis, to work on new material. Marco even had the idea of us starting our own music publishing company. We spoke about it quite often, but never followed through with the idea.

Whatever we were going to decide regarding the future of Fly, it would have to be put on the back burner for a while, as an unusual job offer had come my way. I had been offered a job with Katch 22, performing family shows on a P&O cruise ship. The work would take me away for the whole of Easter and the summer.

I broke the news to Nigel from Lasso the Moon and he seemed ok about it, but I never did rejoin the band upon my return. I didn't feel I could dedicate enough time to the band, what with all the acting work that was coming in. It was different with Fly, because I had no live dates to consider.

The cruise ended up taking me to the Caribbean, Norway and Mediterranean. It was a great job and only involved four hours work a week. We would run three, one hour theatre workshops, during which we'd enrol kids to take part in the show. The week would then end with the actual performance. One of the shows was *Treasure Island* in which I played Long John Silver.

We really did have a free run of the ship and all the port days were days off for us, so I got to see places like Grenada, Barbados, Bergen, Lisbon, Dubrovnik, Rome, Venice and Pisa.

I can remember the theatre company having a day off in St Lucia. We were strolling along a beach, when we found a coconut. We must have spent about half an hour trying to crack it open on a rock, but we just couldn't do it. All of a sudden a stranger came running along the beach waving a machete. No one had a clue what his intentions were, but he just grabbed the coconut and with one downward swoop, split the coconut in half and then left.

During a stop off at Barcelona, we were walking past the department store El Corte Ingles, when I said to my colleagues, "Hey, we should see if they have a copy of the Fly album."

They said they'd help me look for it, though deep down I think they thought I was making the whole 'album' story up. We were all rifling through the music section, when suddenly it appeared in all its glory. Even I was surprised to be honest. I took a picture of it on the shelf and everybody seemed suitably impressed.

Upon my return to the UK my good friend Pete, from Negative Equity Theatre Company, phoned me up for a chat. During the conversation he said, "You know Martin, I really think you'd benefit from attending drama school."

I wasn't sure quite how to take this at first. After all, I was getting regular theatre work. However, what he said made sense. He told me that the intensity of specific actor training may help me to take my career to the next level.

I decided to obtain a prospectus from the Birmingham School of Speech and Drama, with the intention of trying to gain entry onto a postgraduate course. The course was £10,000 for the year.

After discussing it with Jayne, she came to the conclusion that it might be money well spent, if it would later lead to even more work. She suggested that we could remortgage the house. I wasn't sure. It was a lot of money and I'd already spent so much time studying. I just thought my time would be better spent actually working.

I found out that the drama school were offering a few scholarships. So I said to Jayne, "Ok, well how about if I audition anyway? I might not even get in, if I do, then let's take it from there." She agreed and I auditioned in January 2003.

One of my audition pieces was the monologue from Berkoff's *Agamemnon*, which I had performed at university, the one which featured the martial arts routine. I thought it highly unlikely that many people would audition with a physical theatre piece and that this might work in my favour. Sue Hay coached me prior to the audition, to make sure my monologues were as good as they could possibly be.

Nerves are a funny thing. You may eventually get comfortable performing in front of a theatre full of people, but as soon as the environment changes, it can throw you off kilter, like auditioning for drama school in front of just two people in a cold white, empty room.

I was saying to myself, 'Relax, you can do this'. But the more I thought about it, the more nervous I seemed to get. I had been earning money from acting, but what if they didn't want me at their drama school? What would that say about my ability?

After the audition, I had a general interview, but the tutors gave absolutely nothing away.

"Thanks for attending the audition Martin. You will get a letter in the post."

## Hang the DJ

Whilst awaiting a response from drama school, a local DJ named Imran Kahn asked me if I'd be interested in DJing Friday nights at the Little Civic pub, which was situated on North Street, Wolverhampton.

The Little Civic was part of a group of three music venues, which was owned and run by Wolverhampton City Council. The largest being the Civic Hall which had played host to some amazing concerts throughout the years. Morrissey's first ever solo concert had taken place there in December of 1988. Admission to the concert was free to anyone who was wearing a Smiths t shirt. Thousands turned up for the concert, but unsurprisingly, a lot of fans were left disappointed. Demand far exceeded the supply.

Initially, my club night was supposed to be a warm up to Cheeky Monkey, which was an 80s night that took place at the Wulfrun Hall. Imran knew that I had a good knowledge of 80s music, and had told his boss that I would be the ideal person to put on a decent night.

I was determined to make the night as cool and hip as possible, so avoided the cheesy side of the 80s.I decided to call the night 'Blitz' after the famous 80s Covent Garden club that had been at the forefront of the whole New Romantic movement.

The original Blitz club was hosted by Steve Strange and its resident DJ was drummer Rusty Egan. The two would later become part of the 80s band Visage.

Apparently, Steve used to work the door at Blitz and wouldn't allow access to anyone who hadn't made an exceptional effort on their appearance. He once turned Mick Jagger away for being too 'rock and roll'!

Steve also appeared in the video for my favourite David Bowie song, 'Ashes to Ashes'.

I got to meet Steve at a Visage show at the O2 Institute, Birmingham in 2013.

My friend Thu was selling their merchandise.

I had turned up with a rare press photo of Steve from the early 80s. I thought it would be a good thing to get signed. When Steve saw the photo, he seemed genuinely surprised. He couldn't even remember having it taken. He told me that the girl in the photo was an ex-girlfriend.

After signing the picture, he went to hand it back to me, but didn't seem to want to let it go. I pulled at it a couple of times, but still he held onto it. "Do you want the picture?" I asked.

"I would love it. Do you mind?"

"No, you can have it."

He gave me a big hug, ran to the stage and said to his band mates, "Look, Martin just gave me this photo."

Steve Strange was such a warm and generous guy, but unfortunately died in 2015 of a heart attack whilst in Egypt.

My DJ set featured the likes of David Bowie, The Cure, The Associates, The Smiths, Teardrop Explodes, Human League and Visage. Also the more obscure bands like The Mobiles, B-Movie and Classix Nouveau.

As time went on, the club started to attract a wider, more diverse audience, so the music had to cater for these people too. My 80s night slowly turned into 80s/90s then eventually it was pretty much a case of anything goes. Always good music though.

In all my years working as a DJ, I can say without doubt, that Oasis was by far the most requested band. This used to wind me up. There's a whole world of music out there and yet the younger clientele just wanted Oasis. I mean don't get me wrong, Noel has written some good songs, but when you have to hear them EVERY Friday night for about 5 years, well it does start to grate on you....well it did on me anyway.

I had a group of thirtysomethings who used to come to the venue. They used to request bands like The Go-Betweens, The Field Mice and Ride.

I played them all of course, quite refreshing it was too. But then one evening an Oasis fan whose eardrums apparently were being offended, came over and asked, "What the fuck's this shit mate? Stick 'Supersonic' on." The offending song had been The Go-Between's 'Bye Bye Pride'. It was only a blooming classic.

One night someone came up to me and asked, "Mate, what's this song that's playing?" It was 'There is a Light That Never Goes Out' by The Smiths. I remember thinking to myself, 'Oh man, if he hasn't heard The Smiths yet, imagine all those amazing songs he's about to discover, lucky bugger!'

Once a group of girls came up to me and asked for 'Dancing Queen' by ABBA. I just told them straight ... "If I play ABBA, it will clear the dance floor and I may even get sacked, or lynched, or both."

"Go on...PLEASE!"

"No, I can't, I've got Liam Gallagher lookalikes relying on me here."

"Just once, just for us, go on."

"I can't, honestly. If I do, the next group of people will be requesting 'Panic' by The Smiths."

"What!?"

I had no idea why I made the 'Panic' comment to this girl, who hadn't got a clue what I was insinuating. I had to explain.

"You know, hang the DJ hang the DJ hang the DJ."

She hadn't a clue and just walked away.

If I ever needed the toilet, I would always put on New Order's 'Blue Monday' which is over seven minutes long, because it always gave me time to get to the loo and back.

The door lock on the toilet cubicle was always broken, so was very rarely closed. I once went into the toilets and there in the cubicle was this guy on his knees, snorting cocaine off the top of the toilet seat. I just stood there looking at him. Eventually he looked up at me, "Do you know who I am?" I asked.

"No," he replied. "I am the DJ, I work here!"

I was expecting him to apologise, pack up his gear and leave, but he just carried on. After glancing at me again, he asked, "Do you want some?" I stood there for a few seconds dumbfounded, but thought about it and then said, "Yeah, go on then." So I knelt down with him and snorted two long lines.

My circle of friends had never done cocaine. It was always amphetamines. Cocaine was always so much more expensive than speed and in Wolverhampton, it was always referred to as the 'rich man's drug'.

I would go on to have cocaine every once in a while. Actually, one of my good friends, Ian Davies (not to be confused with my brother) was also a Wolverhampton DJ. He used to work later than me, so after I finished my shift, I would go and stand with him for the rest of the night. Ian is a top DJ, specialising in Funk, Soul and Motown.

Anyway, Ian would often get free cocaine. I guess the public just loved him that much. He would put lines of cocaine on a CD and shout at me, "Come on then Davo!" I never did need much encouragement.

Unlike speed, I always managed to sleep after cocaine, this was a massive plus point, but to be quite honest, the novelty of drugs was starting to wear off.

******** 

In March 2003, I got invited to see a Smiths cover band at The Robin music venue in Brierley Hill, which is in the borough of Dudley. I can remember being quite reluctant, because I wasn't really into the whole cover band thing.

I eventually got my arm twisted into going, and was accompanied by my wife, her sister Dawn, brother-in-law, Craig and a couple of their friends.

The place was packed and when the support act came on I really did feel sorry for him, because the noise in the venue was horrendous. The support was a solo artist and he'd got the challenge of trying to cut through the noisy crowd, armed with only his voice and an acoustic guitar. It wasn't easy.

To be honest, I was really attentive, because his voice was amazing and his songs were really interesting. Not only that, but his guitar technique really stood out. I don't want to generalise, but a lot of singer/songwriters don't tend to be great guitarists. A lot of them play chords with a strumming technique, which is fine of course. But this guy was finger picking complicated chord structures and progressions, all the way up and down the neck. It was very impressive.

After that night, I never really thought any more about it. Then about a month later, I was DJing the Little Civic, when the guy walks in with his girlfriend. I recognised him straight away. Well you couldn't really miss him because he was about 6'4" tall.

I just had to go over and let him know how much I enjoyed his set.

I approached him and said, "Alright mate, I saw your set at The Robin, it was great. I really enjoyed it." He seemed pleased that I had remembered him.

"I'm Martin, nice to meet you."

"I'm Scott," he replied.

"If you ever do any recording, I'd love to hear it. I am working here every Friday."

"Ok, no worries."

Then I went back to the decks.

A few months later Scott came into the Little Civic again and handed me a CD. It was a demo of songs he had recorded in his bedroom.

I could never usually sleep straight after getting home from DJing, I always needed an hour or so to wind down, so I played the CD from start to finish. The songs were amazing. In all, there were twelve tracks on the CD.

I didn't really get much sleep that night. I couldn't get the recordings out of my mind. I felt so privileged that such an amazing talent had pretty much turned up out of nowhere and presented me with such a beautiful work of art.

*Dorothy Purcell Junior School music class. Mick Biddulph is on the far right of the back row. I am on the middle row, third from the left. (photo: unknown)*

*Darlaston Comprehensive School's production of The Wizard of Oz. I am second from the right. (Photo courtesy of Express & Star)*

*Attic Studios, with my newly acquired Kawai K1 synthesizer circa 1990.*

*Sunny Daze circa 1991. (Left to right) Paul Martin, me,*
*Paul Cashmore, Ade Beddow and Steve Moxon.*
*(photo: Jackie Reeves)*

*Press ad for "Butterfly Evolution".*

*Flyer featuring the Sunny Daze logo.*

*Twister. (Left to right ) Me, Paul (Lewi) Lewis, Craig (Johno) Johnson and Rob (Jacko) Phillips. (Photo: Unknown)*

*Johno and me on stage at 'Live and Loud in the Park',
Telford.*

*Graduation day 1997. (Left to right) Richard Goodall,
Claire Hand and me. (photo: Alan Davies)*

*Owen Lewis and me in a still from The Dumb Waiter.
(Photo: Unknown)*

*My moment of madness with Jim Rose, Edinburgh 1999. (photo: Geraint Lewis)*

*Me working on the Fly album at Artisan Studios, Birmingham. (Photo: Marco Thomas)*

*Artisan Studio during the 'Put the Needle Down and Fly' recording sessions. (From left to right) Marco Thomas, me and Gary Ainge.*

*Album cover for Fly's, Put the Needle Down and Fly.*

*Still from the play, Silence. Gabby Meadows playingYmma and me playing Eadric. (Photo courtesy of Birmingham School of Acting)*

*Silence, featuring Darren Daly as Ethelred and me as Eadric. (Photo courtesy of Birmingham School of Acting)*

*Scott Matthews signing his recording contract with
San Remo Records in Penn, Wolverhampton. Marco
Thomas looks on. (Photo: Martin Davies)*

*Scott Matthews on the right, with radio DJ Mark
Radcliffe at 6 Music. (Photo: Martin Davies)*

*Scott Matthews with BBC Radio 1 DJ, Jo Whiley.*
*(Photo: Martin Davies)*

*(From left to right) Scott Matthews, Dave Grohl and*
*me, during Scott's support shows with Foo Fighters.*
*(Photo: Sam Martin)*

*The Scott Matthews tour bus outside Wolverhampton's Civic Hall. (Photo: Martin Davies)*

*Scott's sold out show at Shepherd's Bush Empire. (Photo: Martin Davies)*

On tour with Snow Patrol in Germany 2007. (Left to right) Jayne, Gary Lightbody and me. (Photo: Scott Matthews)

*Scott clutching his Ivor Novello award with me looking pleased as punch.*

*A beautiful day in New York City. (Left to right) Scott Matthews, me and Marco Thomas. (Photo: Unknown)*

*Scott Matthews with Radio DJ and TV presenter Dermot O'Leary. (Photo: Martin Davies)*

*Me with music icon, Ray Davies. (Photo: Sally Matthews)*

*Scott playing the Acoustic Stage at Glastonbury 2009.*

*Scott Matthews sings with drummer Sam Martin in the back ground. Cropredy Festival 2009. (Photo Martin Davies)*

*The 'Passing Stranger' video shoot. (Left to right) Sam Martin, Marco Thomas, Danny Keane, Scott Matthews, me and Craig 'Johno' Johnson.*

*Recreating a classic album cover. Abbey Road, London. (Left to right) Scott Matthews, me, Marco Thomas and Pete Sangha. (Photo: Unknown)*

*Me with 80s icon Steve Strange. (Photo: Jayne Davies)*

*The Filmonics, Future Forest album cover.*

*Me and the wife, Jayne Davies.*

# Act 2

# Chapters:

*Demo from heaven and the Birmingham School of Speech and Drama*     133

*Come on, give us some Sex Pistols*     143

*Passing Stranger*     147

*Zane Lowe and the tidal wave*     151

*Columbia Records, "What happened to the ice cream?"*     156

*Island Records*     160

*On the road, from London to Texas, via France and Germany*     174

*The 52nd Ivor Novello Awards*     189

*Britain's Got Talent*     194

*And so 2007 comes to an end.....*     201

*'Elsewhere' and the first bombshell*     207

*MOJO Honours List 2008*     215

*If you are having a chair, I am having a fucking chair!*     219

*The Nick Drake, John Martyn tributes and One Shot Not*     225

*The Sea-change*     233

*Filmonics*     240

*That was then, this is now*     245

### *Demo from heaven and the Birmingham School of Speech and Drama*

The first time I saw Scott play a headline show was at the Varsity in Wolverhampton. I asked my wife to come along, but she was tired and said she'd come along next time.

I remember getting home after the show and telling her that she had missed a truly magical gig. I was one of only five people in the audience, but for me, it felt life changing, the sheer fact that there was a musician from Wolverhampton, who in my opinion had the potential to be up there with the greatest songwriters of all time. And yes, I know that's a bold statement.

The songs on Scott's demo were listed thus:

Scott Matthews "A Passing Stranger".
1. Blue in the Face
2. Dream Song
3. The Fool's Fooling Himself
4. Bottle Fed Blues 1
5. Glitter Kiss
6. Passing Stranger
7. Elusive
8. Firewalker
9. Prayers
10. Shallow Rain
11. White Feathered Medicine
12. Bottle fed Blues 2

The recording was really eclectic and innovative. Its styles ranged from bottleneck blues to classic folk and songs were sometimes followed by a musical interlude, examples of which were the tracks 'Bottle Fed Blues 1' and 'Firewalker'.

Scott had even created his own percussion by hitting a jar with a pen. It was a classic example of a truly innovative artist who was prepared to utilise all the things around him, including everyday objects.

I could hear a whole plethora of influences within his music, including Nick Drake, acoustic Led Zeppelin, Mark Bolan and more contemporary artists such as Chris Cornell, from the band Sound Garden.

Initially, I never even considered giving Marco a copy of Scott's demo. I guess the main reason being the fact that I had never really thought of Marco as a massive singer/songwriter fan. He is of course. One of his favourite artists is Joni Mitchell.

I just wasn't sure it would be to his taste.

When I did eventually play the demo to Marco, the first track I played him was 'Elusive'.

I said, "Marco, you have got to listen to this track, it would be an amazing single."

The track wasn't even half way through, when Marco replied, "Let's make an album with him."

Just like me, Marco had been blown away by 'Elusive'. The song started with the most catchy guitar intro that consisted of a repetitious harmonic guitar riff. Although the song didn't have any drums on it, only simple percussion, it still had a fabulous drive and rhythm to it and at 3 minutes and 40 seconds long, it was the perfect length for a single.

I made Marco a copy of the demo and almost overnight he became obsessed. He would constantly be on the phone to me saying, "We have got to work with this guy." Then negativity and self-doubt would creep in and he'd say, "We've got no chance of working with this guy, he's going to be snapped up."

I think Scott had appeared at a time when Marco needed something new in his life. I am not saying Marco was in the throw of a mid-life-crisis or anything. I just think he felt like he was in a bit of a rut and saw Scott as a possible way out.

It was slightly different for me, because I had finally heard back from drama school, informing me that I had won a scholarship.

Scott's demo got exactly the same response from everyone that heard it. It's funny, because when you have been playing and listening to music for years, you just know when you are listening to something of quality, you just know it. You develop this ear. I guess it's very similar to avid sports fans that can recognise talent in a sportsman, or fans of art or photography, who simply know without question when something or someone is great.

I even played Scott's demo to some of my drama school colleagues. I just wanted to promote Scott's music to as many people as possible.

The students on the post-graduate diploma course were all lovely people. I was worried there might be some egos, but there weren't.

We also shared the building with the students on the three year course. They were nice too, when they weren't running along the corridors singing songs from the musicals. This can go from mildly irritating to VERY irritating, depending on how much sleep you have had the night before.

My two closest friends were Gabby Meadows and Darren Daly. Darren and I actually shared a kiss. It was part of a drama exercise. I was wearing nothing but jodhpurs at the time ... ah the things you do at drama school.

135

Darren is a big football fan too, so we had plenty of banter. Although he is an Arsenal fan, so I guess he had the one-upmanship on me, because Wolverhampton Wanderers are nowhere near as good as Arsenal.

He actually came up to Wolverhampton years later, in 2010, for the Wolverhampton v Arsenal game. My team lost 2-0.

Darren came to the game with a relation. I told Darren ahead of the game, not to come up in any Arsenal colours, as the plan was to have a few drinks and a catch up before the game. I was waiting for them to arrive, when in the distance I could see two figures heading towards me. When they finally came into full view I could see that between them, they were wearing Arsenal scarves, shirts, hat and an Arsenal coat. I had a feeling that making our way through town was going to be like walking the gauntlet...and I was right. At least I had my Wolves shirt on, which may have just saved us from actual physical violence. That said there was still plenty of verbal abuse thrown towards my Arsenal buddies.

We didn't get to have any drinks. No surprise there, so the three of us sat outside the ground until kick off.

Gabby and I are like two peas in a pod when it comes to sense of humour. We still stay in touch, but she lives in Norwich, so it's hard to meet up for a coffee and a chat. I miss our chats.

Gabby has a beautiful voice, which lends itself perfectly to classical theatre and radio. It is also in stark contrast to my very broad Midlands accent. In fact, if my memory serves me correctly, one male and one female were selected from our course to take part in a national radio competition.

A shortlist of names was put forward and Gabby was selected.

It was great that the three of us got to perform our final drama school show together. It was in a play called *Silence* by Moira Buffini, in which Darren played Ethelred (King of England) Gabby played Ymma (princess of Normandy) and I played Eadric (Ethelred's bodyguard).

By May 2004, drama school was over. It culminated with a showcase at Soho Theatre, in London. This is where all the students get to perform in front of agents, to show off their acting ability. Only a handful of actors get taken on by successful agents, and getting a good agent can be the difference between success and failure. A well connected agent can get you into a lot more castings. Whereas to have no agent at all, well then you are often fighting over the scraps, and you end up auditioning for things like theatre in education. Not that there is anything wrong with that at all. But I had already done my fair share, so television work was the ultimate goal.

I only had one offer after my showcase and it was from a terrible agent, whose contract I naively signed. With nothing else on the table, I thought I may as well just take the chance.

Just by sheer coincidence, the first casting he sent me to was a TV ad for P&O cruise ships. The agent called me up. "Can you swim?" he asked. "Yes, I am actually a very good swimmer," I replied. "Good, I will email you the brief. The casting is at Crystal Palace in London."

Upon receiving the brief, I noticed that you had to audition in Speedos, not swimming shorts. My wife found this hilarious. Mainly because I was now 34 years of age and she knew before I had even ventured out to buy a pair that it wasn't going to be a good look for me.

I got myself down to Crystal Palace and was directed to the changing rooms. I started placing my clothes in a locker, when a tall figure appeared right next to me. As I turned to look, I saw what can only be described as a complete Adonis. He looked like one of the cast of the Australian soap opera, Neighbours. I suddenly felt very ill. It got even worse once he'd taken his top off to reveal a perfect six-pack. His body was more than a match for my 34 year old hairy-pigeon chest torso.

Once I made my way to the poolside it got even worse. There was a whole line of hunks. 'What the fuck am I doing here?' I thought to myself. My only saving grace would be my swimming ability. The audition involved being filmed diving off a starting block and swimming half the length of the pool.

I was standing amongst all the other actors and I swear it must have looked like some kind of comedy sketch, where Rodney Trotter from *Only Fools and Horses* accidentally ends up in a swimming competition.

I did my audition. The dive was good and so was my swim. It was all over in a couple of minutes and then I was on the train home.

Suffice to say, I didn't get the job and didn't really think for a minute that I would.

The final straw came when I got sent to an audition in London for a classical play. When I turned up, the casting director said, "You are not Scottish?"

Although highly inappropriate, I laughed out loud. "No," I replied.

"We are only casting Scottish actors."

"I'm from Wolverhampton, you can probably

tell."

"Well I could hear your Scottish accent, but we are only really auditioning Scottish actors. Do you want to read, now that you are here?"

"No thanks."

"Ok, well you take care now."

And that was that.

Now if you are an aspiring actor and you are ever in this situation, and are given the chance to read, you MUST read, because you never know, you might just get the part.

Unfortunately, I had no Scottish accent in my armoury.

After parting company with the agent and wondering what on earth I would do next. I got a call from Marco. He told me that our producer friend, Jon Cotton had heard about a music management course being run by South Birmingham College and it was taking place at the Custard Factory in Digbeth, Birmingham.

The course was one day a week and was being run by two experienced music managers, John Mostyn and Geoff Pearce.

John had managed The Beat, Fine Young Cannibals and Ocean Colour Scene and Geoff was still managing the singer Ruby Turner.

Marco and I immediately enrolled on the course, as we thought it would give us a valuable insight into the mechanics of the music industry.

The course touched on aspects of the music industry that Marco and I had no previous knowledge of, such as management contracts, recording contracts, publishing contracts and the various royalty collection societies, like PPL (Phonographic Performance Limited), PRS

(Performing Right Society) and MCPS (Mechanical-Copyright Protection Society).

To be honest, before attending the course, I didn't even know that there are two types of copyright:

1. The copyright in the song (words and music).

2. The copyright in the actual sound recording.

This is why artists sign a record deal and publishing deal. So for example:

If I write a song on a piano, I automatically own the copyright in the words and music. If someone then pays me to record that song, then that person owns the copyright in the sound recording, but NOT the words and music, if that makes sense. However, I could then sell the copyright in the words and music to a publisher, if I so wished.

Many musicians like to retain the rights to their own songs, and not sell them to a publisher. The publishing side of the music industry generates the largest amount of income, especially in this day and age, when CD sales are at an all-time low.

Of course, there are ways of signing with a publisher and still retaining the rights in your song. This is called an administration deal. The publisher will not own the copyright and only deduct a small percentage of the song's income that is generated. This is usually 10%.

There are all sorts of deals that can be done and I certainly don't want to turn this into a music management manual. There are enough of those on the market already and written by people far more experienced than me. So I will swiftly move on.

As Marco and I were spending more time together, we spent hours discussing the possibilities of working with Scott and what our particular roles would be.

Marco suggested that I should be Scott's manager and that he should be the label. To be honest, I had zero interest in being a music manager. But then, I had no capital to contribute to the setting up of a record label either.

Marco used to worry that if a big shot manager came on board, he would not really want Scott to sign a record deal with a new label, a label with no track record. I could certainly see the logic in this.

It took Marco quite a while to convince me to manage Scott, but in the end I agreed to do it. All we had to do now was pitch our ideas to Scott and hope he liked them.

Marco decided to call the record label San Remo and had everything in place, including a contract, now we just needed Scott to sign the deal, and that wasn't easy.

Scott had got to know me quite well, but now Marco was on the scene and Scott seemed really reluctant to commit pen to paper. We ended up having numerous meetings, where we'd really try and twist Scott's arm into signing the contract. It seemed to take an age to conclude the deal.

Quite a few of the Wolverhampton promoters were aware of Scott, but no one had ever offered to help or manage him. That did surprise me a little. It also made Marco even more paranoid. He'd say stuff like, "Someone else is going to swoop in and offer to work with him." I would say, "Marco, they won't." I for one was well aware that nothing happens that quickly in the Midlands and certainly not in Wolverhampton, where you would often find very high levels of apathy.

Scott eventually signed a recording contract with San Remo Records on 11th November 2004. It wasn't exactly a glamorous affair; he signed the contract in the back garden of my house in Penn, Wolverhampton. No champagne, just bottles of Stella and a CD player spinning the best of Small Faces. Oh yes, us West Midlands folk certainly know how to push the boat out.

Scott signed the management contract the following year and it felt like a truly monumental moment. Pulse Music Management was finally born. We had set the wheels in motion and none of us had any idea where it might lead. I am not even sure we actually cared. We just wanted to help Scott release his album. We let everything else rest in the lap of the gods.

## Come on, give us some Sex Pistols

I started 2005 with my newly acquired music manager head on, spending hours on the phone, calling venues and promoters. I also registered on other artists' blogs, such as, Rufus Wainwright, Damien Rice, David Gray, Tom McRae, Jack Johnson and Stephen Fretwell. Anyone I could think of really. I would join the blog then plug Scott's music... "If you like this, you will love Scott Matthews." It definitely directed a lot of traffic to Scott's website.

We were desperate to get gigs, and our main focus was to keep the shows local. I had recalled memories from my time spent in Sunny Daze, taking all those laborious trips down to London, always with this naive notion that 'London's where it's at.' In my eyes, it was important to try and develop a local following. My thought was that if any music industry people from outside the Midlands were interested, then they would just have to come to us.

Throughout January and February Scott played at a variety of venues including The Glee Club, Birmingham, of which Wolverhampton stalwart promoter and friend, Markus Sargeant was in charge of bookings; Katie Fitzgerald's, Stourbridge; Marr's Bar, Worcester; Chestnut Tree, Birmingham; The Broadway, Stourbridge and Red Lion, Stourbridge.

Scott was playing these shows solo and we didn't always get an attentive audience. There is nothing worse than trying to listen to one person with a guitar, when you have a group of people chatting. It's really annoying.

As well as booking shows, we also advised Scott

to play a few open mic nights, where literally anyone can turn up on the night and play a short set. One of these was The Bull in Moseley, Birmingham.

Marco and I spent the first half of Scott's set desperately trying to keep a group of people quiet who were standing at the bar.

Marco would go, "Sssssshhhhhhh!"

Then I would go, "Ssssshhhhhh!"

They didn't even clap at the end of each song, so Marco and I were trying to make up for it by really going over the top with claps and whistles. Then right at the end of Scott's set Marco came out with the loudest whistle I have ever heard. It actually hurt. I grabbed my right ear with my hand.

I shouted out, "Fucking hell Marco!"

"What?" he replied.

"That was so loud. It's really hurt my ear."

"Sorry Mart."

We approached the bar to thank the guys for talking through Scott's set. But it fell on deaf ears. One chap just responded with, "I don't see what all the fuss is about. He isn't that good. I've heard it all before."

I couldn't see the point in even trying to fight Scott's corner, especially with people who were half cut. Although I did think that if he had listened, instead of talking all through the set, he may have had a different opinion.

Scott packed up his equipment and we left. When I got inside the car, I could hear this buzzing in my right ear and it was even worse when I got into bed that night. I ended up having the noise in my ear for a good few years. In fact, it may still be there, I am not totally sure. Perhaps I just don't notice it as much anymore.

My father suffers with tinnitus, due to years of working in a factory. When I told him about my problem, he said, "Yes, it definitely sounds like tinnitus."

"Great. Is there a cure?" I asked.

"No, but you can learn to live with it."

Marco and I decided to promote our own show at The Station in Birmingham. The event was called, 'An Amazing Night of Acoustic Music' yes, a bit long winded I know. However, the night sold out and was a great success. There were four acts on, with Scott as the headline act. The night was going really well, when suddenly halfway through Scott's set, a loud voice shouted, "Sex Pistols!" I started to scan the room, when above the crowd of heads I saw a full on multi coloured Mohawk hairstyle. How bizarre. This guy must have just wondered into the gig without a ticket. We hadn't employed any security, as we didn't really think we'd need to. I mean come on, how many rooms get trashed at acoustic shows?

Scott started to sing another song and about a minute in … "Sex Pistols!" Now at this point, I was wishing I had kept my martial arts weapons. I really could have done with that blow pipe.

As Scott's manager I was coming to the realisation that I and I alone would probably have to deal with this situation. I told myself that I'd wait until the end of this song to see if he shuts up. But he didn't, he got worse, like he had some form of punk rock tourettes.

"Pistols, come on, give us some Sex Pistols. Sing some Pistols."

I had never seen Scott angry before, but he suddenly stopped playing and shouted, "Just shut the fuck up and fuck off, go on, fuck off!"

The punk just muttered something under his breath, then stood up and left like a naughty school boy, and that was the last we saw of him. Scott managed to diffuse the situation without anyone getting hurt. Good man.

It did play on my mind for the rest of the night though. How on earth had he arrived at our show? And perhaps he just genuinely wanted to hear some acoustic Sex Pistols. I wondered to myself if anyone had ever turned up at a Sex Pistols show and constantly shouted, "Nick Drake, give us some Nick Drake."

Two years later I would be in a position to ask Johnny Rotten that very question, when I found myself standing right next to him, as we both relieved ourselves in a urinal at the MOJO Honours Awards.

## *Passing Stranger*

Scott started recording his debut album *Passing Stranger* at Artisan Studios, Moseley, Birmingham, on 2$^{nd}$ March 2005. To be even more precise, the very first computer file created for Scott's album, was time-stamped at 10:44 am.

Artisan seemed like the logical place for Scott to record the album, as Marco and I had recorded the Fly album there and had got along well with the owner, Jon Cotton.

Jon was at the helm for *Passing Stranger* and would be credited as producer, engineer and mixer, whilst Scott would be credited as co-producer.

Scott's Passing Stranger demo had been a complete solo affair, however, the re-recording would feature a host of guest musicians, including world renowned tabla player, Sukhvinder Singh Namdhari, who had performed with the Indian musician Ravi Shankar. He had also played on legendary guitarist Ry Cooder's 1993 album, *A Meeting by the River*.

Jon knew of Sukhvinder through SAMPAD, the South Asian arts organisation based at Birmingham's MAC arts complex.

Scott also brought in friend Matt Thomas to play drums. Matt is a great drummer and although he only played a handful of shows with Scott, he would later go on to become the drummer in the successful alternative rock band, Joy Formidable.

Marco and I would attend the studio sessions every few weeks. We were really conscious of not wanting to get in the way and to be honest, whenever we did attend, everything that we heard

147

sounded wonderful.

It certainly wasn't all plain sailing though. Half-way through the recording Scott lost his voice. It wasn't something that was rectified with a few days' rest either, and Scott ended up seeing a throat specialist who upon examination with an endoscope, found a reddening of the vocal chords. This came as a relief, as there was fear that Scott's symptoms could have been caused by throat nodules, which are small growths on the vocal chords. These can become quite serious and lead to a permanent hoarseness of the voice and loss of vocal range.

Scott hit a bit of a brick wall too, whilst trying to record the song 'Elusive'.

I got a call from Scott saying that it just wasn't working. This was a real concern, as Marco and I saw 'Elusive' as the possible flagship single.

Scott and Jon really worked hard on the song and then one day out of the blue, I received another call from Scott. "We've sorted 'Elusive'. We decided to slow it right down, and we have done away with the harmonic intro." I must be honest, this made me quite nervous. The intro and tempo of the song were vital elements to its catchiness.

Marco and I got ourselves straight down to the studio to listen to the newly recorded version. It's funny because Jon was trying to explain what had been done to the song, explaining that the instrumentation had been stripped right back and the tempo reduced, but it didn't really put my mind at ease. However, when Jon started the track, my heart skipped a beat. The intro had been replaced by a slow pulsating single-note drone the size of a house, it was quite haunting, but it still managed to sound as catchy as the old intro, and when Scott's vocals came in, well then I knew. I just remember thinking that they had struck gold.

The album was finished around October 2005 and was mastered by Ray Staff at Alchemy studios in London. Ray had made quite a name for himself with a string of classic albums he had previously mastered, which included Led Zeppelin's *Physical Graffiti*, Supertramp's *Crime of the Century* and The Rolling Stones' *It's Only Rock 'N Roll*.

Passing Stranger cost around £9000 to record, including payments to session musicians. The album artwork was designed by Scott and featured a variety of photos taken by his girlfriend, Sally Connolly. We literally spent a night walking the streets of Wolverhampton and had pictures taken of Merry Hill flats and Penn Road Cafe, now Penny's Cafe.

The album track listing did differ slightly from the demo, but the classic songs were all there, with a few additional gems too, such as 'Eyes Wider than Before' and 'Earth to Calm'.

Marco got the CD manufactured and we set a release date for 13th March 2006, with an album launch set for Sunday 12th March at The Varsity in Wolverhampton.

The album would be distributed by Proper Music Distribution.

Tickets for Scott's album launch were like gold dust. Wolverhampton is a small city, and word had started to spread throughout the music community, that a local guy had recorded a debut album and that it was beginning to make waves.

On the launch night, the crowd were spilling out of the main room and into the corridor. It was crazy. Little did we know that it wouldn't be long

149

before things would get a whole lot crazier.

I had been approached by Mick Griffiths, a live booking agent working for a company called Asgard. No other live agent had contacted me at this point and Mick seemed really passionate about Scott's music. Mick represented such esteemed artists as Ocean Colour Scene, Julian Cope, Joanna Newsom and another favourite of mine, Mogwai.

Three months later Scott was supporting Foo Fighters on their two acoustic shows at Regent Theatre, Ipswich on the 12th June and Apollo Victoria Theatre, London on the 14th June.

The Foo Fighters' frontman, Dave Grohl is such a nice bloke. He was so welcoming and couldn't do enough for us. He stood by me during Scott's set with a glass of wine in his hand, and when Scott started playing the song 'The Fool's Fooling Himself', Dave turned to me and said "Man, this is a rock song."

"You need to hear the recorded version, you'd love it," I replied.

'The Fool's Fooling Himself' really is a rock song, and wouldn't have sounded out of place on a Sound Garden album. It remains one of my favourite songs from Passing Stranger.

I have to say, there were moments when I was talking to Dave Grohl, where I just kept thinking to myself, 'Man, you were in fucking Nirvana!'

Mick began to throw a lot of shows our way, and from that moment on Scott started gigging much further afield. He also got to play his first festivals, including Latitude Festival, in Suffolk and Green Man festival, in Wales.

## Zane Lowe and the tidal wave

Initial reviews for *Passing Stranger* were mixed. The Sun, Uncut, MOJO and Word all gave decidedly average reviews. However, some of the regional press and online reviews were much better. MSN Entertainment called it a 'contender for album of the year'. Manchester Evening News gave the album a glowing 5 star review. Indie London, This is Nottingham, Megastar and Subba Culture all gave the album 4/5.

I guess this was my first real wake-up call. I didn't think anyone would have a bad word to say about the album. I thought it was a masterpiece.

We all agreed that the first single off the album should be 'Elusive' and set a release date of September 2006. We then pressed promo CD singles which would be sent to various radio stations.

Marco was trying to find a radio plugger who could work the single for us and whilst looking through Music Week (a trade paper for the recording industry) stumbled across Jeff Chegwin, a freelance radio plugger who had worked in the business for many years and promoted the likes of Paul McCartney, Elvis Costello and Billy Bragg.

Jeff began touting 'Elusive' around the UK radio stations and it wasn't long before a few stations came on board and played the single. Scott was also offered a few live radio sessions. During April and May, airplay and sessions came from Janice Long at Radio 2, Mark Radcliffe at Radio 2, XFM and 6 Music with Tom Robinson.

Jeff's girlfriend, Anjali worked for a production

151

company and offered to help in getting a black and white video made for 'Elusive'. We shot this in a studio in London at a total cost of £5000.

The real turning point came in August, when Jeff got 'Elusive' into the hands of Adam Hudson, who then put it into the hands of Radio 1's esteemed tastemaker Zane Lowe. I recall being in the car with my wife, when her mobile phone rang. It was her brother-in-law, Craig, who just belted out the words, "Zane Lowe's playing Scott on Radio 1!"

Jayne turned to me quite casually and said, "Craig said Zane Lowe's playing Scott on the radio."

"Quick, put the radio on," I replied.

We only caught the tail end of the song, but yes indeed, there it was in all its glory, 'Elusive' on Radio 1.

Zane played 'Elusive' the following night too. It was his 'Hottest Record in the World Today' two nights in a row. Zane explained on air, that he had already made the decision for his hottest record for that day, but had listened to 'Elusive' in the afternoon and changed his mind immediately.

I know it sounds dramatic, but from that moment on, it felt like nothing would ever be the same again. My phone didn't stop ringing. Every major label in the country was contacting either Marco or me. Then there were music lawyers, publishers, booking agents. It's amazing to think that one DJ can have that much influence, but Zane playing the song really was a game changer.

Industry people would travel up to meet us in Wolverhampton. But more often than not Marco and I would travel down to London. We desperately needed a music lawyer on board and these were amongst the very first meetings we had.

Sarah Stennett met us in Wolverhampton. She seemed nice and was really easy to talk to. She is from Liverpool and had a welcoming Liverpudlian accent, however, she was not only a music lawyer, but the founder of Turn First Artists which is a company comprising of a record label, publishing company and also artist management. She discovered and helped break The Sugarbabes.

This made me really nervous. I feared there could be an ulterior motive. Perhaps she was ultimately looking to steal our artist. It was amazing how protective and paranoid Marco and I were by this point.

Sarah is now one of the most powerful women working in the music industry, having played a part in the careers of Ellie Goulding, Jessie J, Connor Maynard and Olly Murs.

We eventually appointed Robert Horsfall as Scott's Lawyer. Robert had 25 years of experience in the music industry, and had acted on behalf of some very high profile artists, including Robbie Williams, Kirsty MacColl and Cat Stevens.

Scott signed a publishing deal with Universal Music Publishing on 28th August 2006. Scott's A&R representative at Universal was Andy Thompson. We'd had a few meetings with Andy and just got along really well.

There was also interest from EMI Publishing, but Scott's lawyer called us one day, to say that EMI really didn't want to get involved in a bidding war with Universal, so that was that.

Incidentally, the biggest company isn't always the best. Universal owns a huge amount of copyrights. The worry is that your artist will get lost amongst the hundreds of others. Smaller publishing companies however, with a smaller roster, can obviously dedicate more time to each artist. Ideally, you want a company that will be both proactive and reactive.

There was another influencing factor with regards to signing with Universal. During a visit to the Universal offices, which are located on Fulham Broadway, London, we noticed framed pictures of The Smiths albums on the wall. I asked, "Do you own the copyright to The Smiths catalogue?"

"Yes," replied Andy. "We have recently acquired them." Of course, strictly speaking, this didn't really mean much at all. But when you are new to the industry, you can often take comfort in such things. Would this really make much of a difference to Scott's relationship with the label? Would the label work harder for Scott just because they owned The Smiths catalogue and we loved The Smiths? Well of course not.

Once the publishing company own the copyright in your work, you just hope that they will work their balls off to get your music used in as many places as possible. This could be anything from television ads to Hollywood blockbusters. The money involved can be huge.

As an example, Scott's song 'Up on the Hill' from his second album *Elsewhere* was later submitted to the director of the movie *Harry Potter and the Deathly Hallows -Part 1*. 'Up on the Hill' would have been just one of a few songs chosen by the film's music supervisor (the person responsible for locating suitable music for a specific project).

Scott's song didn't get chosen for use in the film, that honour went to Nick Cave and his song 'O Children'. The up-front fee was reported to have been £100,000. Although we felt slightly bitter, the blow was softened by the fact that both Scott and I are big Nick Cave fans. You win some, you lose some.

Some good synchronisations would eventually be obtained, 'City Headache' was used in a French aftershave TV ad, 'Eyes Wider Than Before' was used in an episode of US show *Ugly Betty* and 'Elusive' was used in Idris Elba's TV drama, *The Pavement Psychologist*.

At this point, we still hadn't done a deal with a record label, mainly because there was a long queue of record labels vying for Scott's signature and we didn't want to make the wrong decision.

We weren't spoilt for choice on the publishing front, so that was easier. But now we were attending meeting after meeting. Often the labels would be giving it the hard sell, trying their hardest to say the right things to get Scott to sign with them.

I can't remember exactly how many meetings we ended up having, but it was a lot. It felt like we were surfing on a tidal wave that we had no control over, you literally just had to hang on for dear life and hope that at some point you would end up on a nice beach somewhere with a sun lounger and a cocktail in your hand.

## Columbia Records , "What happened to the ice cream?"

One of the first A&R record label representatives to meet us was a chap called Mark, from Columbia Records. We had arranged to meet him at Tottenham Court Road tube station in London.

As Marco and I arrived, we were trying to spot Mark amongst the crowd. The only person I could see that looked like he might be waiting for us was this small man carrying a satchel. I say man, but he looked more like a boy, he looked about fifteen years of age. I said to Marco, "Surely that's not him."

He was wearing a short Harrington style jacket and had a dark, mop-top hairdo.

Suddenly the chap looked me straight in the eye, I smiled and then he smiled. He came over to us and asked, "Are you Martin?"

"Yes," I replied. "And this is Marco."

We all shook hands and then I said, "Or as we are more commonly known, M&M."

I think the joke went over Mark's head, as he didn't even smile. Actually come to think of it, it's not much of a joke is it? Then again, I have used it many times in the past and it has succeeded in raising at least a smile.

The strange thing about this meeting was that there didn't seem to be much substance to the questions Mark was asking. He didn't really talk about Scott's music, but seemed more concerned with who else was interested. I began to lose count of the amount of times he asked this question.

"Thanks for meeting me. Who else is interested? Not that I need to know or anything, but are there many other people interested? You don't have to tell me like."

"Quite a few," I replied.

"You don't have to tell me any names."

We didn't tell him any names. To be honest, he irritated me slightly. I waited to hear Mark's vision for Scott's music and what he thought Columbia could bring to the table. But instead, he seemed more concerned with the competition.

Mark asked us if we'd be up for going out for an informal meeting/meal with the Columbia Records staff. This sounded like a good idea, as it would give us a chance to meet everyone from the label, and I suppose on a basic level, see if we all clicked.

Two days later I received a call from Mark, telling me that we would be going to an Italian restaurant in Camden, London, called Marine Ices. One side of the restaurant serves traditional Italian food and the other side is an ice cream parlour. Marco is half Italian, so I am not sure if this was the motivation behind the choice of restaurant.

Mark assured me that the ice cream was mind blowing. He told me it was the restaurant's unique selling point. London is a huge city. But apparently, if you want ice cream, Marine Ices is the place to go.

I had really built the ice cream up to Marco too. Quite strange, how even in adulthood, you can still get really excited about such simple pleasures, like ice cream.

Quite a few people from Columbia turned up for the meal. As well as the record label boss, whose name I can't quite remember, there was in attendance, Mike Pickering, who had worked for Factory Records and signed the Happy Mondays. That impressed me a lot.

157

I later found out that he had also played saxophone in the band M People, this did not impress me.

After everyone had finished their main course, the head of Columbia lost a ring off his finger. He must have been fiddling with it and the ring had dropped onto the floor. He proceeded to look under the table, then eventually got on his hands and knees. This seemed odd. I don't know why, but it did. The head of a major record label crawling around the floor of a restaurant. Then one by one, we were all crawling on our hands and knees, searching for it.

All of sudden, someone belted out, "Found it." The label boss then got up and asked for the bill.

One by one all the label staff left, with a "Nice to meet you, hopefully speak soon."

I looked at Marco and shook my head.

"Are you thinking what I'm thinking?" asked Marco.

"Yes," I replied. "What happened to the ice cream?"

Scott came out with, "We could just buy some ice cream."

"No fucking way!" I replied. "I have had a lengthy phone conversation about how good this ice cream is and how Columbia would like to treat us to the best ice cream in town and they have buggered off without getting us any."

So, we put our coats on and left the restaurant. Then I began to rant, all tongue in cheek of course.

"I am right though, all we hear about is how fucking marvellous this ice cream is and then they don't even buy us any ice cream. Well they can get lost, Scott you really don't want to sign with them. There is no honour there."

Marco chipped in with, "I wasn't really feeling it

anyway."

Then Scott says, "I know what you mean, not sure I like them either."

All was quiet for a brief moment, when suddenly I broke the silence, "I know Scott, let's make a major decision on your music career, based purely on the fact that Columbia didn't buy us any ice cream."

## *Island Records*

Louis Bloom was another A&R guy that had appeared on our radar. He worked for Island Records. Now in this moment, I have to pay tribute to Island Records. To me, this was no ordinary label. When you look at the label's history and roster, well it is second to none. I could almost just mention Bob Marley and stop there. But if I did, I would be leaving out the likes of Roxy Music, Nick Drake, John Martyn, U2, PJ Harvey and Tom Waits, to name but a few.

We had a few meetings with Island Records. On one occasion, we had met with Ted Cockle (head of marketing) and Ted Cummings (head of press) in the West End of London. After coffee they invited Marco, Scott and me back to the Universal building, situated on High Street, Kensington.

I was sitting next to Ted Cockle in a cab, and he had noticed that I had an image of Bob Marley set as my mobile phone screensaver.

"Bob Marley!" said Ted.

"Yes," I replied.

"This is so the right label for Scott," Ted belted out excitedly.

I was quite annoyed with myself, because I didn't want to give anyone at Island Records an angle they could use to try and influence our decision to sign with them.

All we wanted from any label was honesty and transparency. But it is a fact that most labels will try and sweet talk you. As much as I would have loved to hear fascinating tales about Bob Marley, the most important question we wanted answered was 'What will your label do for Scott?'

When there is a massive buzz about an artist, it

becomes a competition between all the labels to try and seal the deal. After all, if an artist becomes really successful, there can be vast amounts of money to be made.

I didn't fully embrace Bob Marley until my mid-twenties. I mean, I loved the *Legend* album, which is a best of, but I hadn't heard any of his studio albums. The first album I actually bought and loved was *Catch a Fire*, which was the first to be released on Island Records.

Bob Marley eventually became a bit of an obsession and as well as buying most of his studio albums, I went on a pilgrimage to visit Bob Marley's grave with my wife.

Bob's mausoleum is in Nine Mile, St Anne's Bay, Jamaica, which was also his birthplace. It takes about an hour to get to Nine Mile from the coast in Ocho Rios, but it's a beautifully scenic drive through the rural Jamaican countryside.

When you actually see the tomb, it's hard to believe his body is in there. It's just a bit surreal, the fact that you are feet away from the remains of an absolute musical icon.

I nearly didn't make it back from Jamaica. A few days after the Bob Marley trip, I was sailing a catamaran in the sea near Ocho Rios. I had only been out for around twenty minutes, when the weather took a turn for the worse.

I had a total lapse in concentration and turned the catamaran without releasing the sail. Releasing the sail allows you to safely make a sharp 180 degree turn, but what I had effectively done, was turn the taught sail parallel to the wind.

The catamaran flipped instantly. I was thrown from the deck and landed less than four feet from a reef. I had swallowed sea water and was totally disorientated. If I had hit my head, then I don't think I would have lived to tell the tale, because I was bobbing around in the water for at least fifteen minutes, before the sailing instructors came to my aid.

It took four of us to flip the catamaran back over and when I eventually got back ashore, I found out that Jamaica was about to be placed on hurricane alert, as Hurricane Dean was expected to hit in the next 24 hours.

This wasn't my first near death experience at sea. When I was about six years old, my parents had taken me on holiday to Paignton, Devon. We were going to spend a few days on the beach and my uncle gave me his rubber dinghy, so I could happily bob around on the water.

I can remember the beach being really overcrowded. This was the mid-seventies and long before the popularity of Spanish package holidays. This was a time when British holiday resorts were booming.

Anyway, my dad plonked me in the dinghy and returned to sit on his towel. I was only feet away from the beach, but in seconds the current just swept me right out to sea. I was holding on to the plastic rings, where the oars usually go. I began crying as the beach started to get further and further away.

My most vivid memory of that day was seeing my dad running into the sea in his jeans and t shirt, screaming, "Stay in the boat!" He tried to swim out to me, but he couldn't, the tide was too strong.

The next thing I can remember is being rescued by a boat. It wasn't the coastguard, but a sailor who had seen me in danger. Back at the caravan my dad burst the dinghy with a knife and threw it away.

Island Records' then president, Nick Gatfield had dangled a huge carrot in front of us. He had offered to press and release 'Elusive' as a 7" and CD single, with no strings attached. It was a sign of his good will and the label's commitment.

I liked Nick, because he seemed to be a really genuine, down to earth sort of guy. I was also impressed by the fact that he'd played saxophone in Dexys Midnight Runners. He would occasionally irritate me though, by referring to the *Passing Stranger* album as *Passing Strangers*.

Island had put a record deal together, and I met with Scott's lawyer to discuss the terms of the deal. I was new to recording contracts. Yes, I had previously signed a deal with Elefant Records for the Fly album, but I hadn't really paid much attention to its details, well none of us had. We didn't really care that much at the time, a record label had offered to fund our album, and that was good enough. We didn't even contemplate getting a lawyer. By the way, having a lawyer doesn't necessarily mean you won't get ripped off.

There are plenty of examples throughout history of musicians getting ripped off. They get offered a recording contract and are so excited about the fact they are going to get an album released, that they don't pay any attention to the contract.

There have been plenty of unscrupulous managers around too.

A good example of how messy things can get is to look at the legal issues surrounding The Smiths recording contract. The band consisted of Morrissey, Johnny Marr, Mike Joyce and Andy

Rourke. Apparently, only Morrissey and Marr signed the contract.

Years after the band had split up Mike Joyce sued Morrissey and Marr, on the basis that he believed he was entitled to 25% of the band's earnings. However, the contract didn't state that Mike was going to get 25%. This should have been dealt with before the deal was signed. Mike probably didn't even question it at the time, but someone should have. Why didn't anyone question the fact that the contract for a four piece band only had two signatures on it!? I smell a rat.

Mike Joyce and Andy Rourke were not session musicians. They were full-time members of The Smiths.

We were dragging our feet that much over the decision on whether to sign with Island, that Marco and I got a request to meet the head of Universal for UK and Europe, Lucian Grange.

I received a call from Louis Bloom. "Martin, Lucian Grange would like to meet you and Marco for a chat. Lucian very rarely meets anybody, so this is a big deal."

There are two lifts in the Universal building and only one of them goes all the way to Lucian's floor. I used to laugh and say to Marco, "You know you've made it when you've got your own lift."

When I first set eyes on Lucian, he really did appear to be the stereotypical music mogul. Smartly dressed in a white shirt with tie and braces, holding one of the largest cigars I have ever seen. He was sat behind what looked like a very expensive oak table in a very large comfortable leather chair.

The first words he said were, "Take a seat gentlemen."

I felt really nervous. Everything that was going on just seemed to be getting more and more surreal. I remember thinking, 'What the fuck am I doing here? I am from Moxley for fuck sake!' I just felt really out of my depth.

I got even more nervous, when the following words left Lucian's mouth:

"I want you to think of all the countries in Europe as doors." There was a pause and then he leaned forward and said, "And I've got all the fucking keys. I don't care which of my labels Scott signs with, I just want you to make sure it's a Universal label ok?"

He continued to tell us how important Scott was to Universal, and that he'd do everything within his power to put Scott on the map.

"So he will be a priority artist?" I asked.

Marco just looked at me, as if to say, have you been listening to anything he's been saying? Which of course I both had and hadn't.

Because Scott was under contract to San Remo Records, any potential deal would be a licensing deal. This basically means that San Remo (the copyright owner) would licence Scott's album to the new label.

Robert Horsfall was going through the key points of the contract with me.

The contract was a two firm deal, which meant that Island Records were committed to release a second album, regardless of how well *Passing Stranger* did commercially.

After long deliberation, Scott, Marco and I came to the conclusion that Island Records would be the best label to release Scott's music and we set a date for the signing of the contract, which was to be 9th November 2006.

The signing almost didn't take place, because of

a practical joke that very nearly backfired. The contract was going to be signed in a West End pub. Now, I had this ridiculous idea to play a practical joke on Island's Louis Bloom. The band U2 had recently switched labels from Island to Mercury. Both labels are part of the Universal Music Group. I have no idea what went on with U2, but I assume their decision to move labels was to do with personnel, perhaps an ally of theirs had moved over to Mercury and they followed.

I said to Scott and Marco, "Hey, let's play a prank on Louis. Let's tell him Scott's decided not to sign with Island, because U2 have left the label."

Scott and Marco agreed and as we all sat down around the pub table, I made the announcement:

"Louis, Scott's decided not to sign with Island, because U2 have left the label. Scott's a huge U2 fan and this was the only reason he wanted to sign."

"What!?" Louis replied.

Marco's lawyer, Peter McGaughrin was also present and completely unaware of the prank. He didn't look impressed.

Louis began to lose it, "Is that right Scott?" His voice gradually got louder. "Well what the hell are we all doing here?" Then he started to gather his things.

It was time for me to diffuse the situation and reveal it was a not-so-funny practical joke. However, Louis losing his temper had riled Marco, who proceeded to tell Louis "No, we are not doing the deal."

I turned to Marco, "Ok mate come on now." But Marco was like a dog with a bone. I had a feeling this was going to end very badly, when Marco suddenly cracked a smile and everyone breathed a deep sigh of relief.

The contract was signed, we ate some lunch and then Louis and the lawyers left, leaving Marco, Scott and me to ponder. "Do you think we took that a bit too far?" I asked.

Scott replied immediately, "Yeah, I think so."

Marco replied, "Don't worry about it."

We left the pub and I felt a bead of sweat run down my forehead. I kept thinking about all the time and effort that had gone into the meetings with both Island and the lawyers, plus the work that had gone into drawing up the contracts. I told myself from that moment on, I'd try to be a bit more professional. There is a time and a place for jokes, and that was neither the time nor the place.

The last quarter of 2006 was pretty hectic. 'Elusive' was getting quite a lot of airplay from radio stations, including XFM, 6 Music, Capital, BBC London, 5 Live and Radio 2.

BBC radio 1 DJ Jo Whiley loved the song and invited Scott to perform at a few of her university tour dates.

I have to state at this point though, Radio 1 was never fully on board. Their opinion was that *Passing Stranger* on the whole was more of a Radio 2 record.

They thought it would appeal to a more mature audience.

I don't really think this was a valid point. All I know is this; lots of young people were attending Scott's shows. Not just the so called, 'mature', more discerning members of the public. Anyway, surely this is doing the youth of the UK a great disservice.

The following single release was pencilled in for 11th November 2006 and 'Dream Song' seemed to be the most popular choice. The song had a much bigger sound than 'Elusive' and featured lush strings and tabla drums. It was certainly an eclectic sounding song and definitely something a bit different for radio.

The song would be accompanied by a music video shot by up and coming video directors Karni and Saul. The video was shot using stop motion photography and the final result was really effective. The video features a bunch of actors who get out of bed and then perform morning tasks, like cleaning their teeth and getting dressed etc. It doesn't sound terribly exciting, but the way it was shot just makes it work. The whole video is very dreamlike, with bathroom sinks and glasses filling up with water, without anyone actually turning on the taps or filling the glasses.

Reviews of the song were very positive. It got single of the week in The Guardian. It was Zane Lowe's 'Hottest Record in the World', received airplay on Radio 1, XFM, Radio 2 and 6 Music and got play listed on most the student radio stations around the country. The video was also play listed on the MTV2 and VH1 TV channels.

2007 would kick off with the third single from the album and it was Island's decision to release the title track 'Passing Stranger'. A great song, but Marco and I were not keen on this being released at all. We just couldn't see it doing well at radio, but Island Records really wanted to release it, so we went along with it, placing our trust in them, just assuming they knew best.

The video for 'Passing Stranger' was a disaster. Lyrically, the song conjures up images of being on the open road. As clichéd as it may sound, I had an image of Scott carrying his guitar, thumbing a lift on the Pacific Coast Highway. But instead, we had the band and extras dressed in period costume, sharing an opium pipe in some kind of early nineteenth century drug den!

Marco and I were in the video too, but you really didn't even have to blink to miss it.

I have no idea how the video treatment got signed off to be honest, everyone had taken their eyes off the ball with this one, myself included. I don't know anyone who actually liked the video, well I think the video commissioner did, but then she probably had to like it, or that would have been some serious egg on face.

I couldn't see any of the music channels playing the video and they didn't. Not only that, but Marco and my instincts were correct regarding radio too, as the song was pretty much shunned and didn't make any of the national playlists.

Ah that wonderful moment when you are awaiting the results of a radio station's playlist meeting, only to find out that your song didn't make the A, B or even the C list and you have to settle for spot plays (this is where the odd DJ plays your track once or twice on air) which never really has much impact.

In these situations you have to pick yourself up, dust yourself down and move on. We still had the re-release of the album to look forward to and with a major label behind it, well what could go wrong?

********

Island Records were taking care of the UK and European release of the *Passing Stranger* album, but we also needed a releasing label for North America and we were steered towards Universal Republic. Island Records has a history of passing their acts on to this particular label. Some of the

Island artists who released on Republic included Amy Winehouse, Mika and more recently Florence and the Machine.

The label is based on Broadway in New York and as it happened, I had booked a holiday to New York with my wife, brother and his girlfriend, so Nick Gatfield asked me to schedule a meeting with Universal Republic while I was there.

My brother asked me if he could attend the meeting.

"No you can't."

"Why not?"

"Because it's not appropriate, is it?"

"I know but I want to see how you handle it. You know, listen to what you say."

Inside I was saying to myself, 'If only you knew... I have no idea what I am going to say.'

I am sure my brother just assumed I had turned into this music guru overnight.

The truth of the matter is I was terrified. Everything that was going on, well it really was a baptism of fire. Steep learning curve is an understatement.

By sheer coincidence, my hotel was within walking distance of the Universal Republic office. My contact at the label was A&R representative Justin Eshak, whose doppelganger was the Canadian/British tennis player Greg Rusedski.

Justin told me he had ordered breakfast and led me into a lounge area, which was filled with chairs and a central coffee table, which was covered in bagels, muffins and cups of coffee.

I sat waiting for the Republic entourage to enter the room and eventually one by one, they filed in.

I met the following people:
Tom Mackay (A&R)

Kim Garner (Marketing and Artist development)
Bill Richards (Marketing)
Joel Klaiman (Promotion)
Avery Lipman (senior Vice president)
Monte Lipman (President)

It was pretty full on to be honest. Most of the industry people we had met in the UK had been quite laid back, but in the US it was slightly different. Americans are not backwards in coming forwards and they all came at me one hundred miles an hour.

The first words out of Bill's mouth were, "Man, you have no idea how long we have been waiting to meet you, we are so excited about Scott Matthews and his *Passing Stranger* album, it's wonderful."

Again, it felt like a barrage of well-rehearsed industry clichés, designed to win me over. But you have to put your trust in someone. Being constantly suspicious doesn't really get you anywhere.

By the way, it wasn't the first time I had met Justin Eshak and Tom Mackay. Justin came to see Scott at a show in Birmingham and Tom came to a show in Portsmouth. Scott was only a couple of songs into his set at Portsmouth, when he accidentally knocked over a glass of red wine that had been placed on top of his amplifier. The entire contents of the glass seeped into the amp and it cut out immediately. It seemed to hold the show up for an extraordinary amount of time.

Not the level of professionalism you want, when you have important industry people in the audience.

Marco, Scott and me would end up making a few trips to New York for various meetings, not only with Universal Republic, but a whole host of music industry people.

One big question we asked ourselves was whether we needed a US manager. It would be difficult for us to coordinate everything from the UK, so someone on the ground in the US, fighting Scott's corner, could be really advantageous.

We met a lovely guy called Gary Waldman from Morebarn Music. His company manage both artists and producers. We were all big fans of singer/songwriter Ryan Adams and Morebarn managed Neal Casal (Ryan Adams' then guitarist).

One of the most bizarre meetings we had was with the agent Jeff Frasco from Creative Arts Agency, based in Los Angeles. They represented musicians, actors and sportspeople. Footballer David Beckham was one of their clients.

Jeff's secretary kept calling my home phone, trying to arrange a meeting. I was working out of an upstairs home office, so my wife would normally answer the phone as it was downstairs. I always told her to put on a nice 'phone voice' in case anyone important called.

Jayne would answer the phone with a polite "Hello?" And if it turned out to be an industry person, she'd say, "Yes, Martin is available, I'll just put you through." Then I would run downstairs and take the call.

The first time I ever heard Jeff's secretary on the phone, I almost burst into laughter. She sounded exactly like Rosemary, the quirky police station telephone operator from the 70s cartoon *Hong Kong Phooey*.

Marco and I eventually got to meet Jeff over breakfast in a New York hotel. Jeff was a very busy guy...he conducted the entire meeting with a bluetooth earpiece firmly lodged in his ear. I am not sure if this was supposed to be sending us the message that he is on the ball, always available and ready to take calls, or that he literally was always available and ready to take calls. Either way, it just didn't seem like the right fit.

## On the road, from London to Texas, via France and Germany

Island Records were going to re-release *Passing Stranger* in March 2007. This would be preceded by an extensive tour of the UK and Ireland.

We started to assemble a band and crew for Scott's forthcoming shows and the final list was as follows:

Craig 'Johno' Johnson (bass guitar). Yes, this is in fact the Craig Johnson who I'd grown up with. I had introduced Johno to Scott, they got along like a house on fire. Johno auditioned and got the job.

Sam Martin (Drums). Sam was from Stoke and had turned up at Paolo Nutini's show at The Sugarmill in Stoke, June 2006. Scott was the support act, and as we were putting the equipment away after the show, Sam approached us and offered his services as a drummer. He is a lovely chap. He auditioned and got the job. Oh, I have to point out that Paolo Nutini is a lovely guy too. Our paths would cross a few more times over the coming years, mainly during radio sessions. Often he would be leaving a radio station as we were arriving or vice versa.

Danny Keane (cello). Born to be a musician. Danny is a magnificent player.

Danny's second instrument is piano, which is frustrating, because I could only dream of playing piano like Danny, and piano is my first instrument.

Jake Willman (monitors). Controlled the

174

onstage sound.

Alex Warhurst (front of house). Controlled the sound in the auditorium.

Damo Fowkes (guitar/drum tech). Damo is the best air drummer I have ever seen. His air drumming to Black Sabbath's debut album really is a sight to behold.

Nicole Latimore (LD). Lighting designer.

Simon Smith (tour manager). Legendary tour manager I might add. Simon had been the drummer in the band The Wedding Present before becoming a tour manager. Simon is a top man and great at his job.

Like it says on the tin, the tour manager's job is to manage the tour. In simplistic terms, the role involves everything from booking hotels and transport to communicating with promoters to obtain get-in times for venues and generally making sure a tour runs smoothly. Touring is an expensive game. Although a tour will often be undertaken to promote a new album, in an ideal world, you will also want to try and make money for your artist. So you want to try and make savings wherever you can, but not to the detriment of the tour of course.

We had decided to use a 12 sleeper bus for Scott's initial 2007 January dates. The bus cost £400 per day. This sounds like a lot of money. However, consider the expense putting 10 people up in a hotel, and you would still need to hire a vehicle to transport the band and equipment.

I have to point out that Danny's cello had its

own bed. I think the cello was made in the 16th century or something and is insured for about £18,000.

On January 12<sup>th</sup> 2007 Scott supported legendary folk singer, Bert Jansch at the Roundhouse in London. Bert had a few guests playing with him, which included Beth Orton and ex-Suede guitarist Bernard Butler. Scott followed this gig with a headline show at Whelan's in Dublin. Then on 22<sup>nd</sup> January Scott, his girlfriend Sally and I travelled to Midem, which is an annual music industry tradeshow, which takes place in Cannes, France.

People attend from all areas of the music industry and new artists can showcase their material, which is basically what Scott was doing. You can also make good business connections.

This was the first time I caught sight of Amy Winehouse. Amy was performing in a room adjacent to Scott's. We actually got to watch her sound-check and her voice took my breath away. I couldn't believe that such a huge voice could come out of such a small person, she was tiny.

Amy's show was later than Scott's, so we got to see her performance, which was truly mesmerising. Her flagship single 'Rehab' had been released on 23rd October 2006 and was followed shortly after by the release of her 2nd album entitled *Back to Black*. It was a fantastic album and put Amy right on the map. It would go on to become a multi-million seller. I was expecting a similar level of sales for *Passing Stranger*.

Now that Scott had signed with Island Records, I just thought the weight of the label would push Scott's debut through the stratosphere.

Scott's headline tour would start on Saturday 27th January 2007 at Colston Hall, Bristol. Simon Smith instructed everyone to meet outside Wolverhampton Civic Hall in the morning. This is where the bus was due to pick us up. The band was super excited. Most of them, including myself, hadn't been on a tour bus before. We were like kids in a sweet shop. We were literally high fiving each other, as we discovered all the features the bus had to offer.

I think Sam was the first person to run up the stairs to check out the sleeping quarters. He shouted, "It's got a Playstation!" The bus had two lounge areas. There was one on the bottom deck, which doubled up as a kitchen area, and there was a lounge upstairs with TV, DVD and a collection of films. The toilet was downstairs, but there was no shower. As we hit the motorway, it all felt quite surreal.

I have to say though, that it didn't take long for the novelty of the tour bus to wear off. Firstly, the bunk beds are not that comfortable and if you are claustrophobic, then you have a real problem, because the bunks are tiny. If it's a windy night, the bus sways quite a lot too, even more so if you are travelling on the motorway at speed. This made me feel quite nervous and I would never really get a good night's sleep.

Bristol was followed by Academy 2, Manchester on the 28th, ABC Glasgow on 29th, Wulfrun Hall, Wolverhampton on 30th and finally a 2000 capacity sell-out show at Shepherd's Bush Empire, London.

This was only the short first leg of the tour. The second leg would begin in March, but before that Scott was due to tour Germany, supporting Irish band Snow Patrol.

Snow Patrol's lead singer, Gary Lightbody, had been co-hosting one of Radio 1's evening shows, when he actually announced live on air that he had been trying to get in touch with Scott, but felt he was being ignored, as he hadn't had a response. I think someone from our record label had given Scott's email address to Gary.

The next morning I contacted Snow Patrol's management and told them that Scott hadn't received the email from Gary.

Snow Patrol was managed by Jazz Summers of Big Life Management. Jazz had managed Wham! The Verve and Scissor Sisters et al. The man was a music industry legend. If you get chance, I highly recommend you get his autobiography, *Big Life*. It's a great read.

Anyway, it turns out that Gary was trying to get hold of Scott to ask him if he wanted to support Snow Patrol on their tour of Germany. The dates were as follows:

February 2007:

4th Stadhalle, Offenbach
5th Heineken Music hall, Amsterdam
6th Stahlwerk, Dusseldorf
8th Theaterhaus, Stuttgart
9th Columbiahalle, Berlin

It was too good an opportunity to miss, so we agreed to do the shows. My wife and I decided to tag along too.

If you know Scott's music, you could be forgiven for thinking that Scott and Snow Patrol is a strange combination, especially considering the fact that Scott would be performing the shows acoustically with his drummer Sam, who would be playing percussion. This was a slight worry, because we weren't sure the sound would be big enough for arena venues; Heineken Music Hall holds 6000 people.

Would Snow Patrol's fans think it was a strange combination too? As it turned out, we had been worrying for nothing. Scott's sound translated well and the crowds really responded to Scott's songs.

Snow Patrol had come a long way. They had achieved a level of success with their 2003 album *Final Straw*, but it was their 2006 release *Eyes Open* that gave the band huge mainstream success. Their career was also given a massive boost by the use of their song 'Chasing Cars' in a key emotional scene in the successful US medical drama *Grey's Anatomy*. After the episode, sales of the single began to soar, giving them a massive foothold in the States.

The Germany tour didn't get off to the best of starts. Simon had rented a splitter van off a friend and its condition was questionable. We hadn't even left the UK, when we discovered the sky light was letting in a huge draft. We stopped at the services and Simon patched up the sky light with some masking tape. I think we had been spoilt by the tour bus and now being in a smaller vehicle with a draft, well it was back down to earth with a bump.

Support acts don't get paid much at all, so you have to budget accordingly.

In fact, we wouldn't have been able to do the tour, were it not for tour support money paid by Island Records.

We also had an incident on the way to Stuttgart. We were on the autobahn during a particularly dark and dismal day with strong driving rain, when all of a sudden one of the windscreen wipers fell off. Simon cool as anything, just pulled over, retrieved the wiper, pulled out a tool kit from the van and fixed it in a matter of minutes. Luckily it was the passenger side, because had it have been the driver's side, the rain was coming down so hard, who knows what might have happened.

It was a wake-up call for me and from that moment on, I made strict rules with regards to vehicle hire. You get what you pay for.

During Snow Patrol's shows, Gary always went above and beyond the call of duty when it came to plugging Scott's album. Every night he would shout to the audience, "Please give a big hand for the support act Scott Matthews, an absolute genius. Do yourselves a favour, as soon as you get home, download his album, it's fantastic."

I cannot speak highly enough of Snow Patrol. They really looked after us on that tour, and were total gentlemen. Snow Patrol I salute you x

On Scott's return to the UK, he had a whole host of radio sessions pencilled into the diary, including Capital, XFM and BBC London, after which we were due to fly to Austin, Texas, for the South by South West Festival.

We were due to fly out on 14th March, but upon reaching Birmingham Airport, we discovered that our connecting flight in Amsterdam had been cancelled. We couldn't find another flight, so I phoned Nick Gatfield at Island Records to break the news. He wasn't happy.

We were driving back to Wolverhampton, when Nick phoned me and said, "Don't unpack, I am trying to sort you a flight." Two hours later, we were driving to Heathrow Airport. We couldn't get a direct flight, and had to change planes at Cincinnati.

Scott was due to play three shows at South By South West; a lunchtime show on Thursday 15th for BBC Radio 2, then an evening show for the Universal Republic label and on the afternoon of Friday 16th, he would play a show at Bourbon Rocks, which was the Island Records showcase.

The line up for the Island showcase was as follows:

The Fratellis
The Rumble Strips
Josh Pyke
Amy Winehouse
Scott Matthews
Mika

For some reason, Mika didn't want to play the show. I have no idea why, but he turned up at the venue with his guitarist, but no instruments.

The venue was packed to the rafters and the atmosphere was electric. Once Mika got a whiff of the electrical charge within the room, he immediately had a change of heart and wanted to play his set.

I just thought he was a prima donna. I had never really liked Mika to be honest, I just considered him to be an extravagant, over-the-top bubblegum pop artist, appealing only to kids and moms. I mean he had a song called 'Lollipop'. Plus, I had heard from label sources that he could be 'difficult'. A fact I was now discovering first hand.

As it turned out, Mika had a very nice manager, who politely asked me if Scott would mind offering a guitar for the duration of Mika's set, and of course Scott duly obliged.

The evening of Friday 16th was going to be a night off, but I got a call asking if Scott would like to play another BBC Radio 2 show at La Zona Rosa. Apparently, the singer James Morrison was stranded in New York due to bad weather. So Scott was offered his 9:30pm slot, just before Amy Winehouse.

We were sharing a dressing room with television presenter and Radio DJ Dermott O'Leary. I had been having trouble with my knee for a couple of days, and was in so much pain as I limped into the dressing room, I never even introduced myself.

Dermott didn't seem to mind, he seemed more concerned about my limp. I suddenly realised my faux pas, "Oh, I'm sorry, nice to meet you. I manage Scott Matthews, who's standing in for James Morrison. I've done my knee in."

It was quite embarrassing. Dermott seemed really nice though and became a huge fan of Scott's, inviting him to perform twice on his Saturday afternoon Radio 2 show.

After Scott's set, we watched Amy Winehouse and then Razorlight. During Razorlight's set, Scott nudged me, "Have you seen who is standing right next to you?"

I turned to look and immediately turned back to Scott, "Fucking hell... It's Spiderman's girlfriend." I couldn't remember her name.

"It's Kirsten Dunst," he replied.

I turned around a couple more times, I just couldn't help myself. It turns out she was dating Razorlight's lead singer, Jonny Burrell.

We had a fantastic time at South by South West

and made some important contacts too, including Frank Riley from High Road Touring agency.

Frank was one of the most straight-talking people I had met in the States, plus I loved the fact that he wasn't a suit. Nothing about his appearance was business-like whatsoever, if anything, he looked more like (and I mean this in the nicest possible way) an aging hippy. He had long hair, wore jeans, a t shirt and had small round rimmed glasses, like a 70s John Lennon.

As for High Road Touring's roster, well they represent some of my favourite artists, including Ryan Adams, Portishead, Television, Wilco, Wild Beasts and Maccabees.

We all quickly came to the conclusion that Frank should take care of Scott's touring in North America.

It is often said, where there's an up, there's a down, and the Texas trip ended on a bit of a downer for me, and this particular fly in the ointment was Murray A Lightburn, from the Canadian band The Dears.

I had been a fan of The Dears, ever since the release of their brilliant 2004 single, 'Lost in the Plot'. Coincidentally, we also shared the same UK booking agent, Mick Griffiths.

We were checking in at Austin-Bergstrom International Airport, when I noticed that The Dears were checking in at the desk right next to us.

Once we had checked in our baggage, we were sitting in the terminal, when The Dears suddenly appeared and sat opposite us. Marco and Scott were both reading books, so I thought I would seize the opportunity and congratulate Murray on their new album, *Gang of Losers*.

Murray was sitting with a Macbook on his lap.

"Hi Murray, I just wanted to congratulate you

on *Gang of Losers,* it's such a great album." Murray, flicked his eyes up from the laptop to look and me, but said nothing.

"I manage a singer/songwriter called Scott Matthews. He is represented by Mick Griffiths from Asgard." I really thought this statement would break the ice.

He said nothing. Well actually, that's not entirely true, because he mumbled something, but I have no idea what it was.

This was one of those moments, when you want the ground to just open up and swallow you. I had congratulated him on his music and he couldn't even be bothered to acknowledge me.

My mind went into overdrive, as I desperately tried to decide how to extract myself from the situation. Do I persevere with the conversation? Do I say goodbye and walk away? Or do I just say nothing and leave? I began to feel the red hot glow of embarrassment expand across my cheeks.

I didn't say another word and turned and walked away. Murray didn't even notice, because by this point his eyes were firmly focused back on his computer screen.

I explained to Marco what had just happened. Marco hadn't heard of The Dears and seemed a little nonplussed. He did however come out with the statement, "Sometimes you find the most famous people are the ones that have the smallest egos."

"Not sure if it's an ego issue. He just seems like a miserable fucker." I replied.

As soon as I got back to England, I called Mick Griffiths and explained what had happened. Mick didn't seem surprised. "Yes, he can be a bit moody."

Shortly after, I found out that Asgard was no

longer representing The Dears. However, I don't think it had anything to do with my phone call to Mick.

I have to confess, I am still a huge fan of The Dears, and still regularly listen to their albums. It may sound pretentious, but I think that great art should be above everything, even the people that create it. When it is out in the world, you could argue that it no longer belongs to the creator. It takes on a life of its own and belongs to the people that embrace it.

In 2013, Murray A Lightburn released a solo album entitled *Mass:Light*. It's a modern classic. Check it out if you get chance. Just don't ever approach him at the airport.

*Passing Stranger* was re-released the day we returned from Texas, on Monday 19th March and Scott was immediately on the road to promote it with the following dates:

March
Wednesday 21st...Carling Academy, Liverpool
Thursday 22nd...Warwick University, Coventry
Saturday 24th...Music Hall, Aberdeen
Sunday 25th...Queen's Hall, Edinburgh
Monday 26th...University of Leeds
Wednesday 28th...Rock City, Nottingham
Thursday 29th...Waterfront, Norwich
Friday 30th...Plug, Sheffield
Saturday 31st, BBC Radio 2 session with Bob Harris

April
Sunday 1st...Brookes University, Oxford
Monday 2nd...Coal Exchange, Cardiff
Tuesday 3rd...Pyramid, Portsmouth

Wednesday 4th...Corn Exchange, Brighton
Wednesday 11th...Spring & Airbrake, Belfast
Thursday 12th...Village, Dublin
Friday 13th...Savoy Theatre, Cork
Saturday 14th April...Roisin Dubh, Galway

Along with the *Passing Stranger* album, Island Records were keen to re-release 'Elusive'. They were certain they could do a job on re-launching the single and wanted to shoot a brand new video to accompany it.

There was an added factor behind Island's thinking, 'Elusive' had been nominated for a prestigious Ivor Novello Award.

The shoot date for the video was Friday 11th May 2007, and it was pretty much going to be a basic performance style video shot in black and white.

The location for the video was Templeton House, in Priory Lane, London, which is a huge gorgeous Georgian listed building.

Templeton House is a stone's throw away from the famous Priory rehabilitation centre, which has seen many a celebrity pass through its doors.

Now it's fair to say that Scott is generally not a fan of shooting music videos, especially if said video involves any miming, which this one would. Oh and not forgetting the nightmare that was the 'Passing Stranger' video, this made Scott even more edgy.

These facts didn't make for the easiest of shoots. I mean, I can see Scott's point of view for sure, no one really wants to mime, but most artists have to do it at some point in their career.

Island wanted Scott to be the main focus of the video because it is important for the audience to connect with the artist, to actually see what the artist looks like and of course, seeing the artist's emotions also helps the audience to connect with the emotional content of the song.

The production company was Draw Pictures, who had been responsible for shooting a number of music videos for the likes of Mark Ronson, Keane and Band of Horses. So this was obviously on a different scale to the first 'Elusive' video, which had been shot on a fairly tight budget and with only a miniscule amount of crew.

We had around twenty five people on set for this shoot. Everyone from director, 1st assistant director, 2nd assistant director, focus puller, clapper loader, grip, gaffer, electricians, I mean you name it. In fact, they even appointed Scott a stylist. Even I thought this was pointless. Scott is a pretty cool guy and has some great clothes. However, Island Records really wanted Scott kitted out in a new suit and even insisted on a new haircut. So measurements were taken and clothes were bought, all falling under part of the budget, of which 50% was recoupable by Island Records.

Music videos can be painstaking things and you can't help but feel for the artist.

If the video is a one-day shoot, you can almost certainly guarantee that it will be a very long day.

Scott was really looking forward to this day being over. However, we had a late afternoon scare. There was a fault with a piece of equipment. I assumed it was to do with the lighting, because a rapid flicker became apparent on the footage, but it had been missed by the director who had been viewing the monitors as the shoot progressed.

The fear was that we'd have to return to re-shoot parts of the video. This would have been a complete nightmare, because there just wasn't much space in the diary. We were due to fly back out to New York, after which we would be in the thick of festival season.

Breaking the news of a reshoot to Scott wouldn't have gone down well at all. I was worried that he may even just refuse to do it. We spent the next thirty minutes analysing the footage and the general consensus was that they could get away with it. We all simultaneously breathed a huge sigh of relief.

## The 52nd Ivor Novello Awards

'Elusive' had been nominated for 'Best song musically and lyrically' at the 52nd Ivor Novello Awards. Scott's fellow nominees were Arctic Monkeys and Nerina Pallot.

The ceremony was being held on Thursday 24th May 2007, at Grosvenor House, Park Lane, London.

On the morning Universal Music Publishing decided to take us to a gentlemen's club for drinks. I placed my usual order of a regular latte, but really could have done with something stronger. It was our first awards ceremony and I was nervous. I can only imagine how Scott must have been feeling.

When the waitress got to Mike McCormack, then head of A&R, he said, "I will have a Long Island Iced Tea please." I wasn't sure if I had heard him correctly at first. Yes indeed, we certainly were new to this scene. I wanted to change my order, but the moment had gone. A Long Island would have been the perfect drink to settle my nerves.

Mike McCormack was a collector of vintage digital watches and had a massive collection. I have a couple too, my favourite being a 1985 Casio DBC-62 digital calculator watch. Mike had shown me his 1970s digital driving watch, which was a real belter. Mike said to me, "Martin, if Scott wins the Ivor Novello Award, I will give you one of my watches."

"Are you serious?" I asked.

"Yes, I am serious."

When we arrived at the Grosvenor and were shown to our table, I suddenly realised that the latte was probably a good call after all, because the table was loaded with booze. Each table had three Ice buckets just packed with everything from bottled beer to fine champagne.

I hit the champagne immediately, hoping it would help me to relax, but it was hard not to feel like a fish out of water. Suffice to say, the drink went right through me, so I went on a toilet finding mission. By the time I reached the toilets I was so desperate, that upon relieving myself I gave out a huge sigh of relief, the kind of sigh you only give when you relieve a bladder that feels like it has blown up to the size of a football.

There was only one other person at the urinals, and my noise must have distracted his concentration, as I got the feeling he was looking at me. I glanced over about to make some kind of apology, when I realised it was Elton John. I nodded, he nodded, and then we simultaneously turned to use the wash basins. I washed my hands as quickly as possible, so I could catch him up. Not to speak to him you understand, but to look at him. Now I know that sounds very weird, but there are stars and there are STARS. I think I just wanted to confirm that it was definitely Elton John, and not just a figment of my imagination.

When I got back to my table, I sat down and exclaimed, "I have just been in the toilets with Elton John." Now when you make a remark like this, it doesn't take a genius to work out what the possible response might be. Ah the human race is so predictable at times.

Elton's was the first of many famous faces spotted at the awards, and at one point during the evening Marco nudged me, "Mart, look who's over there."

I turned to look, "Who is it?" I asked.

"Peter Gabriel," Marco replied. "Let's go and speak to him."

"We can't."

"Why not?"

"Because it's Peter fucking Gabriel."

But then Marco reminded me of a conversation he'd had with our radio plugger Jeff Chegwin. Jeff had said that he saw Peter Gabriel on a plane and that he had heard Scott's album and loved it.

That was all I needed to hear. "Ok Marco, but you lead the way."

So we set off through the crowd and we caught Peter just as he was getting up out of his seat. Marco jumped straight in with "Hello Peter, Martin and myself are huge fans." Peter looked at me, but I didn't speak. I just didn't know what to say. Marco continued, "We work with Scott Matthews, who is up for an award tonight."

Peter replied, "That's great, nice to meet you both." He never mentioned Scott, which left us feeling a bit perplexed and wondering whether he had in fact heard of Scott.

There were so many questions I wish I'd have asked Peter, like did Tony Levin (Peter's bass player) really use a nappy to muffle his bass guitar strings to get the wonderful tone on the song 'Don't Give Up'? But it's one of those things I guess, that when a moment like that takes you by complete surprise, your brain just can't think straight. You have this internal panic set in, where your main concern is making sure you don't come across like a complete idiot. Because if you do, then every single time you play their music from that moment on, it will take you right back to the time where you made a dick of yourself right in front of them.

191

The moment eventually came, when Scott's award category was announced, followed by the moment when Scott was proclaimed the winner. The award was presented by Robin Gibb from the legendary Bee Gees.

Scott gave a lovely speech, thanked all the relevant people and then was whisked away for a few photos.

It's funny, because when Scott's name was announced, Marco and I were screaming and giving each other high fives. He had pipped Arctic Monkeys to the post, which felt fantastic because they are a phenomenal band and I just assumed they'd win.

TV presenter Zoe Ball came over to our table and said, "I love Scott." We were all on cloud 9.

There was a big after show party taking place at a local club and we all went there en masse. When we entered the club there was a small area that had been roped off and we were ushered inside it. However, the only people within this area, was Scott, Marco, myself and the singer Corrine Bailey Rae, whom we politely smiled at.

We had been in this area for about ten minutes, before I turned to Scott and Marco and said, "What the fuck are we doing in here, let's go and mingle." So we left the area and split up into the crowd. The drink had been flowing for such a long time, and I had got to that point where you feel like you have almost drunk yourself sober. I was completely compos mentis and the only thing on my mind was my digital watch. So I went on a mission to find Mike. I eventually found him, held my wrist up and pointed to my watch with a huge grin on my face. He smiled at me, "Don't worry, I haven't forgotten."

192

I don't remember much more about the after show party, but I certainly remember getting back to our hotel and witnessing another very awkward moment.

When you win an Ivor Novello award, they give out two lovely statuettes. One is for the artist and the other is for the artist's publisher. Now we had been escorted back to our hotel by our Universal Publishing A&R representative, Andy Thompson. Once we got into the hotel foyer, Marco asked Andy if he could have a look at the statuette. Andy happily handed it to Marco and then, basically, Marco refused to give it back.

You could see the beads of sweat appearing on Andy's brow. Imagine Andy turning up at the Universal offices next day, minus an Ivor Novello Award.

"Marco, give it him back, it's not your award," I said.

"But I should get one as well," was his reply.

"The award isn't for record labels," I replied.

"Let me just keep hold of it tonight, I will give it back tomorrow."

Scott chipped in now too, "Marco, give it him back."

Just like the Island Records contract signing prank, this seemed to go on for ages. However, this wasn't really a prank. Marco genuinely wanted the award for his mantel piece.

Eventually, Marco handed the award back and Andy went home.

We all laughed hard about it over breakfast the next morning, as we dwelt on what had been a truly magical night.

## *Britain's got talent*

I really wanted to try and grow the management company and for that to happen I needed to find more artists. Although I was busy managing Scott, I was still doing the occasional DJ slot in Wolverhampton. Sometimes I would be DJing downstairs at the Little Civic and there would be a band playing upstairs, so I would put a compilation CD on, so I could catch fifteen minutes of the band's set.

On one occasion, I went upstairs to check out the band and as I walked into the room, I was stopped in my tracks. It was a band called Alterkicks and they were brilliant. The vocalist had got a really unique voice.

I always respect someone that has a great voice, but for me having a unique voice trumps vocal dexterity any day of the week. Voices like Mariah Carey and Whitney kind of wash over me. I appreciate they can sing, but I prefer voices like say, Jim Morrison, Kurt Cobain or Morrissey.

The song I heard when I entered the room was called, 'The Cannibal Hiking Disaster'. The narrative was brilliant. It was basically about two friends that go hiking, when one of them, Jed, has an accident. The friend tries to get help, but is stranded with no food and water, so he decides to eat his friend, but Jed isn't dead and regains consciousness after his friend slices off a piece of his thigh. It sounds quite morbid, but the structure and melody of the song is flawless. It sounded like a potential indie-hit single to me.

Alterkicks ended their set with a song called 'Do Everything I Taught You'. This also sounded like single material. I got quite excited and just had to meet the band. I couldn't let this opportunity pass me by. I ran back downstairs to make sure everything was ok and that my DJ booth was free from invaders.

I tracked down Alterkick's singer. His name was Martin Stilwell and the band was from Liverpool. I complemented him on their songs. He seemed like a really nice guy, but unfortunately nothing could come from meeting them, he told me that they already had management and a record deal. They were signed to B-Unique Records, the label that had signed successful UK band Kaiser Chiefs.

Alterkicks' debut album, *Do Everything I Taught You*, was released in August 2007, but unfortunately the group disbanded shortly after its release. It was such a shame, they had massive potential.

Another band I came into contact with at the Little Civic was a young Wolverhampton band called Bridge 55. Again, they had some great songs and their front-man Joe Karchud was a star in the making. He had such a great look.

I remember the first time I saw them live. Joe was wearing black shoes, skinny jeans and a thin silk scarf. He had bags of energy and his dancing was slightly reminiscent of Joy Division's Ian Curtis.

After getting to know the band, I agreed to help them out. The average age of the band was eighteen and they didn't have a lot of money between them, so I funded a three track demo recording, which they completed at Artisan Studios.

The songs recorded were called, 'Just the Start', 'Something in Common' and 'Mind, She Never

Did'.

Bridge 55 had a strong local following and their song 'Something in Common' was a fan favourite, so I knew they had to record this track.

I started to send the demo out to record labels and organised a showcase gig at The Barfly, London. A showcase is basically where a band performs mainly for industry personnel. Obviously, it helps if the band already has a fan base and in this technological age, record labels will often use social media sites such as Facebook and Soundcloud to gauge the level of an act's following.

If a record label is interested in a band, they will often send A&R representatives to see them play live. There is nothing better than the band playing to a packed out venue, it means there's a buzz.

I remember our A&R rep, Louis Bloom telling me about the band Mumford and Sons. He was saying that he saw them play live a few times, but didn't think they were quite ready for a deal. However, he noticed that with every gig he attended, the audience was constantly growing. Island eventually signed Mumford and Sons and the rest is history.

We had a few record labels turn up for the Bridge 55 showcase, which had been arranged by Scott's agent Mick Griffiths. Bridge 55 was not the headline act, but another of Mick's bands called Effie Briest. This was ideal, because at least the band would be playing to a full venue.

Bridge 55 were new to London, so they were never going to fill the Barfly. But, they could pull a very respectable crowd in Wolverhampton, so to be honest, I was just interested in showcasing the band's talent and potential initially, knowing deep down that if any industry people came to Wolverhampton they'd be suitably impressed by the band's army of fans and this would help push things forward.

I knew the industry people would find a few faults with the band, mainly the personnel. It's funny the comments they come out with, things like, "He doesn't look good." "He seems miserable." Or, "They don't look like a unit."

The band was so young and had big dreams. Imagine yourself as a manager having to tell certain people within the band that they didn't fit in, essentially crushing their dream. It's not a very nice thing to have to do. But that's the role and if it's the difference between the band getting signed or not, well then I suppose those decisions have to be made.

The one person everyone seemed unanimous about was Bridge 55's vocalist, Joe Karchud. Mick Griffiths said to me, "He's a star."

I really believed that too. Joe was such a talented front man. Island Record's Louis Bloom really liked him too, although he didn't like Joe's moustache! I thought it was unique, having a nicely formed moustache at such a young age, he just looked different, but still cool, I thought it suited him.

I passed all the industry comments on to the band once we got back to Wolverhampton. However, I never asked anyone to leave the band and just decided to crack on as we were, for the time being.

A few months after the showcase, the band wrote two new songs 'If There's Ever' and 'Warmer Conversations'. They were both really strong songs, so I decided to send the band back into the studio again.

All of the bands demos were good, but I had this vision of how great the songs could really sound, if they were in the hands of a top producer. But for this to happen, the band would need a record deal. Unfortunately it wasn't to be.

I think Joe probably paid a bit more attention to the industry's comments on the band than I did to be honest, because one day I got a call from Joe telling me he was going solo.

I didn't really see Joe as a solo artist. Plus he would be leaving behind all the Bridge 55 songs that I was so fond of. Suffice to say, things fizzled out. I still like to think of Joe as 'a star in the making'. He is the best front man I have ever seen in an unsigned band. In fact, I'd go as far to say that he is better than a lot of 'signed' front men. I do still hear from him occasionally, which is always nice. Last I heard he was a working at a college, teaching music performance technology.

Marco and I got involved with another local band too, called Kid Captain. They had been playing locally for a number of years and also had a good following. Kristian Jones was the lead singer and the driving force behind the band, taking on the managerial role single-handedly. He'd obtain gigs and send their demo recordings off to record labels and radio stations, in fact he had managed to get Radio DJ Steve Lamacq to play a couple of their songs on air.

I loved Kid Captain's sound, because I could hear the influence of some of my favourite bands within their music. Bands like The Cure, Radiohead and The Smiths. A record deal had always eluded the band, so Marco and I set out to try and change that.

Our first idea was to remarket the band, and give them a fresh start. To do this we advised the band to change their name. Now I have to say that this isn't always the best thing to do, especially if the band has a following. However, Marco and I didn't feel we'd achieve much approaching record labels with an 'old brand' to use industry style terminology.

The band eventually settled on the name Seafields. We invested in new t- shirts, badges, a demo CD featuring new material and lighting for the band's live shows.

We managed to get the band a few gigs, but nowhere near as many as we would have liked. One of the highlights was obtaining a support to the 80s band, Flock of Seagulls, at the Wulfrun in Wolverhampton.

Mike Score was Flock of Seagulls' front man and the only remaining original member of the band.

Seafields played a blistering set and during the interval, Marco and I went around the auditorium handing out free CDs. We had pressed around one hundred and they went in minutes.

I was desperate to get Seafields a live agent and of course my first port of call was Mick Griffiths, from Asgard. However, he didn't really like the band.

Again, we put our efforts into a London showcase, but nothing came from it and the band quickly got disillusioned. We were accused of gathering the wrong industry people for their style of music. Now, I can't completely disagree with this statement, but it's not like we didn't try to get the 'indie' labels to attend. We approached all of the band's favourite labels, including Moshi Moshi, Fierce Panda, Domino and Bella Union.

But at the end of the day, you can't put a gun to their heads and force them to attend.

We eventually reached a point where all we'd do was disagree.

Because we couldn't get any record label interest, we decided to record and release an EP on Marco's San Remo Records label. We could then use this as a good calling card for the band, as it would be an official release.

I think Kristian was into the idea, but Andy, the guitarist was totally against it. In fact, when I asked, "Don't you want to release an EP?" He said, "Yes, but not with you guys."

In a way, it was music to my ears. I wasn't really enjoying managing them. Nothing to do with the band as people I might add, they are all really nice guys. But it had just become such hard work.

I don't think Marco's heart was totally in it either. In those circumstances, you are all just wasting each other's time. We left Seafields behind and I guess in a way it felt like we had failed.

I started to ask myself whether I really wanted to manage anyone else, mainly because it was always such hard work and I would feel terrible if I couldn't get results.

## *And so 2007 comes to an end …*

The re-release of 'Elusive' hadn't had the impact everyone thought it would. Radio pretty much ignored it. Did it feel like 'old news' to them, because it had been released previously? Who knows. It's not like the song had saturated radio the first time around, so I saw no reason why radio wouldn't come back on-board, especially now Scott had the backing of a major label.

The next idea from Island Records was to release a deluxe version of the *Passing Stranger* album. They wanted to redo the artwork, to make it more 'commercial' and wanted to add a second disc to the package, which would feature five acoustic tracks recorded with a string quartet.

The acoustic sessions were produced by legendary producer John Leckie, who had produced a whole host of classic albums, including The Stone Roses' debut album, Radiohead's *The Bends* and The Verve's *A Storm in Heaven*.

The new artwork was designed by Alex Lake, a photographer and designer who had previously done album covers for the band Keane.

Overseeing releases is often quite stressful, with radio edits to be done, artwork to approve and strict deadlines to be met. It wasn't always that enjoyable, what I did love, however, was seeing the energy of a live audience and the festival season of 2007 had been really fruitful. As well as the likes of Cornbury Festival, Latitude, iTunes Festival and Electric Picnic, Scott played his very first Glastonbury Festival, which was an amazing, albeit very wet experience.

Glastonbury 2007 was a particularly wet year

and I found myself wading through six inches of mud water. Scott's sound engineer had flown in from sunny Spain wearing sandals. I thought it would come as a shock to him, but he didn't appear to give two hoots and left his sandals on for the duration of the festival.

I had never been to Glastonbury Festival before, so it did feel slightly strange that my introduction to the festival was not as a punter, but as a manager, working with an artist who was going to be performing to a full crowd on the legendary John Peel stage.

2007 would end with two tours and an appearance on BBC 2's *Later with Jools Holland* show. The first live dates were starting on 24th September and would form part of a club/promotional tour of the States. The tour would open in New York and end in Los Angeles. In between there was Cambridge, Philadelphia, Charlottesville, Chicago, Minneapolis, Colorado and Portland.

I didn't travel to the US and left the tour in the capable hands of Simon Smith, Scott's trusted tour manager.

Marco and I didn't think that a club tour was the best way to introduce Scott to the United States. We thought it would have been a much better idea to get Scott supporting an already established US act, thus playing to a much larger audience. However, Universal Republic was really keen on the idea, so we rolled with it.

The USA is a notoriously difficult nut to crack. By November 2007, Scott's album had sold just over two thousand copies of the eight thousand that had been shipped. The main markets were New York, Los Angeles, Boston, Detroit and

Philadelphia.

Scott arrived back in England on the 11$^{th}$ October, and then on the 13$^{th}$ he was straight back out on the road, this time supporting legendary singer/songwriter, Rufus Wainwright on his UK tour.

Seeing Rufus play live was a really special experience. Rufus comes from a very musical family. His dad is folk singer Loudon Wainwright III and his mother was the late folk singer Kate McGarrigle.

Rufus plays both piano and guitar and his voice is one of the most unique in music. His 2003 album *Want One* is one of my favourite albums of all time.

The great thing about Scott supporting Rufus was the fact that the audience were so attentive and appreciative. This didn't come as a total surprise really, because Rufus has such a sophisticated sound. Generally speaking, only *real* music lovers attend his shows, the kind of audience that love nothing more than to sit and listen in total silence. It's a magical thing to behold.

After the show at Hammersmith Apollo, London on 31$^{st}$ October, we all headed off to Rufus' after show party, which was taking place at a posh London Hotel. The party was being held next to the hotel's swimming pool. We had taken a small entourage with us, including Scott's cellist Danny Keane and his friend and double bass player, Tom Fry.

To be honest, we were all hoping it would be a free bar, but it wasn't. I asked Scott what he wanted to drink and he said he'd have whatever I was having. Scott had worked his socks off on the tour and had earned a double, so when I arrived at the bar, I asked for two double Bacardi and Cokes. The barman said, "That will be £28 please." Well, my jaw nearly hit the floor. I mean £28! You could buy two bottles of Bacardi for that price.

When I got back to Scott, I said "Enjoy that, there won't be another." He asked why and when I told him the price, he was stunned. Neither of us had ever experienced those kinds of prices.

Through the crowd I noticed the singer/songwriter Ed Harcourt. All my friends were fans, big fans actually. I was gutted that Johno wasn't there, because he loved Ed as much as I did. Ed's 2001 album *Here Be Monsters* was nominated for a Mercury Music Award and it's a classic.

In fact, I can't remember the year, but a group of us went to see the band Turin Brakes at the Little Civic in Wolverhampton. We popped upstairs to check out the support act, which turned out to be some bloke we didn't know, playing solo piano, so we went back downstairs to the bar. Turns out it was Ed Harcourt! We never quite got over that one.

At one point Ed came over to say hello to Scott. I went off on one, telling Ed that my mates would all be gutted that they hadn't got to meet him. I told him that my mates referred to him as the UK's most underrated songwriter.

I think he was getting quite embarrassed by my comments, because after he played all these compliments down, he grabbed me, picked me up and tried to throw me in the swimming pool. My feet were off the ground and I called out "No Ed, not the pool, not the pool!" Eventually he put me down and we all saw the funny side.

It was obvious however, that it was only a matter of time before someone ended up in that pool, and of course they did. At one point, I heard all this commotion, then a huge splash. Our friend Tom Fry had stripped down to his underwear and jumped in the pool.

We were willing Tom to get to the other side before security caught him. Not too difficult a task as the pool was only about fifteen metres in length.

Tom managed to swim to the other side, everyone cheered and then security got him out.

We had a brief chat with Rufus before we all left the party. He was a nice guy but was keen to make it clear how lucky Scott was to be doing the support.

"You know, you're so lucky, I have the most amazing audience. They just love music and will sit and listen and not talk, it's simply wonderful."

Rufus is quite a dramatic character. In fact, I can remember walking into catering whilst on the tour and his band members were sitting around a table sowing sequins into their stage clothes. I assume this was compulsory. Imagine that being part of your contract.

So here it was, the final engagement of 2007 and what an engagement. We had lost *Top of the Pops*, *The Tube* and *Whistle Test*. The only really great televised music show left was *Later with Jools Holland*.

The filming date was Tuesday 28th November at BBC Television Centre. Also appearing on the show was Mr Hudson, The Hours, Scissor Sisters and The Good the Bad and the Queen.

Scott would be performing 'Dream Song' accompanied by Danny Keane on cello and Birmingham based tabla player, Manveer Singh.

It was so strange turning up at the film studio. I had been watching the show for years, but to actually be there, it kind of felt like a magician giving away his secrets. The sound in the studio is so small. There is a live audience, but the actual sound is for broadcast, not for the live environment, so depending on where you are in the room in relation to the act playing, means that sometimes all you here is this tiny sound emanating from the very small speakers. I just assumed the volume in the studio would be like attending a rave.

Most of the acts on the day managed to get through their song in one take, but The Hours and Scissor Sisters needed to do multiple takes.

It was a marvellous way to end the year. We all tuned in for the broadcast of the show on 1st December and as well as taking in Scott's performance, Jayne and I were of course watching to see if we could spot ourselves. During the show Jools sits down to speak to musician and presenter Roland Rivron. We could be seen sitting on the table behind him.

## 'Elsewhere' and the first bombshell

The promotional treadmill that was *Passing Stranger* was over and now it was all about album number two, which was going to be called *Elsewhere*.

The recording budget for the album was £100,000 and there was much deliberation about where and with whom it should be recorded. I suggested that Scott should use the money to build his own studio. As long as you deliver an album, you can pretty much do what you like with the money. It's only a loan after all. Once the studio is built, you then have the space and equipment to record all your future albums.

Scott didn't seem keen on the idea, so it was a case of looking at existing studios and producers. John Leckie's name was mentioned at one point, but Scott eventually settled on recording the album in Wolverhampton with Gavin Monaghan at Magic Garden studios. I think Scott liked the idea of a local studio, whereby he could return to his home comforts after a hard day recording.

The recording of the album turned out to be a lengthy process and no other work was undertaken whilst it was ongoing.

During April, Scott was still busy recording when out of the blue I received a letter from Universal Music Publishing. Well to be more specific, it came from their director of legal and business affairs.

The letter stated that Universal was exercising the 'Parachute Option', which meant they were terminating the agreement. Basically, if *Passing Stranger* didn't sell 150,000 copies within the first

12 months of its release, then Universal had the 'Parachute Option' as a get out clause.

*Passing Stranger* hadn't sold anywhere near that figure. By that point I think we were closer to 60,000. Really disappointing sales figures, especially considering the amount of money spent on the campaign. A staggering £350,000 was spent on TV advertising alone.

When Universal Publishing dropped Scott, it had massive implications, because it meant that Scott wouldn't be getting any second album advances (£125,000 on commencement of recording followed by a further £125,000 on release).

From that moment on, most of my daily communication was with Scott's lawyer. He thought there was an argument to contest Universal's termination, because contractually, they should have terminated before Scott had started recording his 2nd album, which they hadn't. That said Robert Horsfall wasn't 100% certain we would win the case if it did go to court.

To be honest, I couldn't even contemplate taking on something like that. None of us could, well apart from Robert of course. What was that ABBA song again? Oh yes, 'Money Money Money'.

There was letter after letter about the possible outcomes of a court case, but as hard as it was to lose the advances, my only thought was to accept Universal's termination and move on. At least Scott would be writing off the existing debt with them and he could start again with a new publisher.

Eventually, everyone agreed that this was the best course of action and so we took it on the chin. But it didn't stop me feeling disappointed at how impersonal it had all been. I had considered our Universal Publishing contacts as friends. However, they turned out to be anything but. I understand it's just business. But to receive a letter from a lawyer, and not even get a phone call from anyone at the label. Well I think that's nothing short of spineless.

Oh and did I ever get my watch? Did I arse.

So Scott was without a publisher, but we still had Island Records on board. Although, that said, they were extremely quiet during this period and notable by their absence when it came to A&Ring the new album. Scott was in the final stages of recording and there was no sign of Louis Bloom, or anyone else from the label for that matter.

Eventually, Louis Bloom did make an appearance and so did Ted Cummings, who was still head of press. However, it was well and truly after the horse had bolted. The album was virtually finished, so they were unable to have any input or influence on the recordings.

The track listing for *Elsewhere* was as follows:
Underlying Lies
Jagged Melody
Suddenly You Figure Out
Fractured
12 Harps
Speeding Slowly
Into The Firing Line
Up On The Hill
Elsewhere
Fades In Vain
Nothing's Quite Right Here

The album cover features a segment from a painting by Bruno Cavellec.

Bruno is a great friend and artist, who Marco had first met at a record fair about twelve years ago. As well as taking some very early photos of Scott, Bruno also made an appearance on the *Passing Stranger* album. He performs the spoken word on the very last track, 'Bruno Finale'.

'12 Harps' had a guest vocalist, in the shape of former Led Zeppelin singer Robert Plant. I think Jimmy Page had heard *Passing Stranger* and alerted Robert about its quality. With both Scott and Robert being Midlanders, I don't think the collaboration came as a massive surprise really, especially considering the fact that Scott was a Zeppelin fan too.

Marco and I went for a meeting with Island Records, after we had sent them the newly finished album. We took Scott's lawyer with us, as we suspected there may be trouble afoot.

The President of Island, Ted Cockle (he had taken over from Nick Gatfield) was looking through the track listing and said, "Yeah, I mean there are a couple of good songs on it." Then Louis Bloom said, "What's that one song now Ted, I really like it?" Ted threw the CD across the room so that Louis could read the track titles. I saw this as hostile and totally disrespectful.

It got worse from that moment, because Ted suggested withholding our final advance, so Island could use the money to help promote the album. Of course contractually he couldn't just do that, he had to ask us if we were OK with it. This is when Robert Horsfall started firing on all cylinders.

"No way! Why should they? Is it their fault that sales for *Passing Stranger* haven't been what you expected?"

Ted was trying to appeal, but it was falling on deaf ears. The thing is, as an artist, if you haven't recouped your advances, then you won't be receiving any royalty cheques, which essentially means that you are relying heavily on the advances.

We couldn't afford not to take the advance. Besides, it was my theory that the label would have retained the advance, and not put a penny of it towards promoting the new album, because first and foremost the label didn't like it.

We left the meeting and deep down I knew that this was going to be the beginning of the end. Island Records were fulfilling their obligation to release the 2nd album, but I knew there wouldn't be a third.

The final album mixes were still to be completed, but they would have to wait, because Scott was about to head off on a tour, this time supporting Robert Plant and Allison Krauss on their 'Raising Sand' tour.

The dates were as follows:
Monday 5th May 2008...NIA, Birmingham
Wednesday 7th May...Apollo, Manchester
Thursday 8th May...CIA, Cardiff
Saturday 10th May...Philipshalle, Dusseldorf
Sunday 11th May...Forest National, Brussels
Tuesday 13th May...Le Grand Rex, Paris
Wednesday 14th May...Heineken Music Hall, Amsterdam
Friday 16th May...Hovet, Stockholm
Sunday 18th May...Spektrum, Oslo
Monday 19th May...Bergenshalle, Norway
Thursday 22nd May...Wembley Arena, London

I flew out for the Amsterdam show and also attended the Wembley Arena show.

I watched Scott's sound-check at Wembley, and

then as I was walking back to the dressing room, I saw a figure in the distance walking towards me, it wasn't until I got a few feet away, that I realised it was Rodger Daltrey from The Who.

The Who's *Quadrophenia* is an album that would easily make my top 50 albums of all time. That said, I didn't speak to Roger, the man is a living legend and perhaps I didn't want to ruin it by experiencing another 'Murray in Texas' moment.

At that time Robert Plant and The Who shared the same manager, Bill Curbishley. So I presume Roger was there to see the show.

After Scott's set at Wembley Arena, Robert Plant and Bill Curbishley came into Scott's dressing room asking who Scott's manager was. I tentatively said, "That would be me." They were quite intimidating. Robert asked if we were getting a good hourly rate at Magic Garden studio, and then said that he wanted to have a meeting at some point in the future, to discuss business ideas.

Marco, Scott and I did eventually have that meeting with Robert Plant and Bill Curbishley at Trinifold Management offices in London. I think Robert was into the idea of doing something with Scott in the US.

Robert gave us a few contacts, one of which was Rounder Records, who are based in Nashville. We were given the details of founder member of the label, Marian Leighton-Levy, but after sending her a copy of *Elsewhere* and chasing her over the course of a few weeks it became apparent that there wasn't much interest. We couldn't really do anything at that time anyway, as Scott was still under contract.

Upon the completion of *Elsewhere*, a release date

was set for May 18th 2009. It was also confirmed that the first single from the album would be 'Fractured'. Again the single would be accompanied by a video.

The idea for the 'Fractured' video was brilliant. It was set in the Wild West, with Scott playing a sheriff in pursuit of a bank robber. Unbeknown to Scott, the fugitive has been thrown from his horse and is hanging off a cliff, with the bag of money in one hand and horse's reins in the other. The only way the fugitive can save himself is to let go of the money.

The one-day shoot took place at Broadway Quarry in Malvern, Worcestershire. The location looked great on film and with the opening sequence, in which a bird of prey circles the quarry, you could be mistaken for thinking it was shot in the States.

I think 'Fractured' is a great song, and although the lyrics are quite ambiguous, the song definitely gives a sense of someone questioning their life and the decisions they have made, with lines about plans blowing away and finding a way out. Was this Scott questioning the decisions he himself had made? I am not sure and never asked the question. There was certainly a lot going on at that time, especially with Island Records, with whom we were feeling quite disillusioned and I am sure they probably felt the same about us too.

I am really fond of the 'Fractured' video, because it was so beautifully shot and captured the essence of the song perfectly. It has long been one of my favourites, second only to Scott's stunning video for his 2014 song '86 Floors From Heaven'.

'86 Floors From Heaven' would appear on Scott's fourth album, entitled *Home part 1*, released in 2014.

The song is about Evelyn McHale, an American woman, who threw herself off the top of the Empire State Building, New York, in 1947. A photographer took a picture of her minutes after the fall. It captures her dead body perfectly preserved on the roof of a car. In the photo she appears to be clutching her necklace. There is no sign of any blood. She literally looks like she's asleep.

On the 86th floor, police found her neatly folded jacket and a notebook containing a suicide note.

The video was directed by Lukasz Pytlik, a Polish film-maker, whose details were obtained from Radar Music Videos. This is a website that connects musicians and up-and-coming film directors. You can post your songs on the website along with your lyrics. You can also state deadlines and budget.

The '86 Floors' video is a masterpiece in film-making. Entirely shot in black and white, the video is made up of free stock vintage footage and also features a young actress playing the part of Evelyn.

There is nothing obvious about the video. It's all very subtle and poetic. The video ends with Evelyn slowly falling backwards, clutching onto her pearl necklace. Her image then becomes superimposed with a theatre audience in rapturous applause.

# MOJO HONOURS LIST 2008

The MOJO honours awards took place at The Brewery, Chiswell Street, London on Monday 16th June 2008. The honours are MOJO music magazine's annual awards ceremony and they had asked Scott to present the Les Paul Award to legendary folk singer John Martyn. Scott is a big John Martyn fan and he was over-the-moon that he had been asked to present the award.

On the day, the plan was to meet Scott's PR representative Ted Cummings in a pub close to the venue, just to kick back and have a catch up for an hour or so.

We had been in the pub for about half an hour when in walks none other than former The Jam frontman, Paul Weller. In fact, he stood right next to me at the bar.

Although my childhood friend Lewi was now slowly trying to distance himself from the rest of us, I couldn't help but think about him in this moment. He was Paul Weller's number one fan. I just wished he could have been there too. He would have loved the opportunity to meet his hero.

On our arrival at The Brewery, the street was lined with photographers and taxi cabs dropping off the various guests. We arrived just ahead of the Welsh singer, Duffy. As soon as she got out of her taxi, the cameramen went into overdrive. "Duffy, Duffy, look here. DUFFY, look here."

The flash from the cameras was disorientating, I had never seen anything like it. We just filed into the venue with no fuss whatsoever and in that moment, being anonymous felt quite liberating, but of course there was a small part of me wishing

215

that the photographers had been calling Scott's name.

Because Scott was presenting an award, we were placed on a table two rows from the front of the stage. Sitting on the table in front of us sat the band The Last Shadow Puppets, to our right, Duffy and ex-Suede member Bernard Butler, who spoke to Scott, as he had remembered him from his gig supporting Bert Jansch. To our left was the Sex Pistols and directly behind us was one of my heroes Nick Cave and the Bad Seeds. I couldn't contain my excitement. "Scott, look it's Nick Cave!"

"You going to talk to him?" he replied.

Now, before I could even answer, Scott's publicist Ted came out with a comment that knocked me off-kilter.

"Nick Cave is a man of meagre talent. I have more respect for Johnny Rotten."

I couldn't get my head around this statement. Ted had been in the industry for a number of years and surely, even if he wasn't a fan, he must be able to recognise a great songwriter when he hears one. To give Johnny Rotten more respect seemed absurd to me, that's nothing against Johnny of course, because we all recognise the importance of the Sex Pistols and their impact on youth culture. They were at the forefront of the punk movement in the UK. And then of course, there was Johnny's post-Pistols band PIL, who garnered a massive amount of respect too.

With that one statement, I had lost all respect for Ted. Calling Nick Cave a man of meagre talent! He may as well have made the statement about The Beatles or The Stones, yes, Nick Cave is that good.

I didn't get into Nick Cave until my early

thirties. I remember accidentally stumbling across a concert on TV in the early 90s. I think the gig had been filmed at London's Town and Country Club, but I am not certain. Anyway, I couldn't really get into it. Fast forward to the year 2000 and I was hooked. If you don't know any of his albums and want to dip your toe into the water, check out the albums *No More Shall We Part* and *The Boatman's Call* as a starting point.

In fact, put this book down right now and listen to the song 'Into My Arms' on Youtube. It's the most amazing piano driven ballad.

As a protest against Ted's statement I stood up and said, "I am going to speak to Nick Cave." The ceremony hadn't started yet, so I decided to strike while the iron was hot.

Marco had spotted the band Genesis across the other side of the room and being a huge fan, he said quite casually, "Right, I am going to have a word with Genesis." As you do.

I was really nervous as I approached Nick's table, having no real idea of what sort of character he was, but I had to speak to him, I just had to. "Excuse me Nick I just wanted to say how much joy your music has given to me and my wife." He shook my hand and said, "That's great, thanks. Where's your wife?" I told him she was working and he said, "Well really nice to meet you." It was a fleeting moment, but it made my night, now I could confirm that Nick was not only a genius songwriter, but a thoroughly nice bloke too.

I would get to speak to Nick again in 2013, at the airport on the way to Bergenfest in Norway. Scott gave Nick a copy of his *What the Night Delivers* album. We even got to see Nick's headline set from the side of the stage at the festival. It was magnificent.

The MOJO Honours was a real star-studded event. Among the nominees were, Radiohead for best album (*In Rainbows*) but they lost out to Nick Cave, who won the award with his album *Dig, Lazarus, Dig!!!* Duffy was up for 'song of the year'. Led Zeppelin for 'best live act'; Paul Weller was getting the 'outstanding contribution to music' award and the Sex Pistols got the 'Icon Award'.

During a break in proceedings, I went to the toilet and found myself urinating next to Johnny Rotten. He was having a right old rant about the Kaftan he was wearing and the fact that it was making it hard for him to access his penis. This made me chuckle. I was tempted to ask him if anyone had ever called out, 'Give us some Nick Drake' at any of his gigs, but of course I didn't.

It was such a beautiful moment when Scott finally got to present the award to John. Scott had written such a lovely speech, mentioning not only John's influence as a songwriter, but as a guitarist too.

Unfortunately, John was now wheelchair bound and the effects of his prolonged alcohol abusive were all too clear to see.

On arrival back at the hotel, we made our way to the lift and discovered that John was also waiting. By sheer coincidence he was staying at our hotel. Scott went to speak to him, but he was so drunk, he didn't recognise Scott at all. It was a crying shame.

Within a year, John would be dead. He died on 29th January 2009 at the age of 60.

### *If you are having a chair, I am having a fucking chair!*

The relationship with Island Records was gradually going from bad to worse and Scott's 'last hurrah' was his contribution to Island Records' 50th birthday celebration CD.

'Island Life: 50 Years of Island Records' was going to be a 3CD box set. The first two discs would feature a collection of songs from Island artists past and present, then the 3rd disc was going to be a collection of Island artists performing cover versions of other Island artist's songs.

I suggested to Scott that he should cover a Bob Marley song. I think Scott's producer Gavin Monaghan had also had the same idea. Scott ended up recording the most sublime version of Bob Marley's classic 'Is This Love'.

Scott's version of the song started with a sitar intro and then went into a lush acoustic version, complete with layered harmonies.

Other notable artists who contributed cover songs, were Paul Weller, who sang Nick Drake's 'River Man'. Keane, who recorded Pulp's 'Disco 2000' and Grace Jones with Roxy Music's 'Love is the Drug'.

Everyone at Island Records loved Scott's version of 'Is This Love'. I suggested that it should be released as a single, but that was met with negativity, as Island felt that it wasn't upbeat enough for radio. I fought and fought, "Yes, but it's amazing, I just know that it will get airtime, it's one of the best Marley covers I have ever heard."

Suffice to say, it didn't get released as a single, in fact, during the coming months, Louis Bloom

219

and I would have a massive disagreement over the song.

Louis suggested that it should go on Scott's *Elsewhere* album. I really wasn't keen on this idea and neither was Scott. Albums are a work of art and putting a cover version on the release, just to try and sell more copies ... well that's diluting the art in my humble opinion. Would it have made a difference to sales had it have been on there? Personally, I really don't think it would have made any difference whatsoever, unless Island was prepared to release it as a single.

The penultimate email I received from Louis on the issue, asked, "So are you saying it's a definite no, with regards to 'Is This Love' appearing on *Elsewhere*?"

I responded with, "Sorry Louis, Scott definitely doesn't want the song to appear on the album."

The final email from Louis just said, "BIG MISTAKE".

The release of *Elsewhere* was somewhat of an anti-climax. I thought it was a great album, but the first two reviews I read were quite damning. Q magazine were virtually saying they had made a mistake praising Scott in the first place and the MOJO magazine review was just as bad. I couldn't understand what these fuckers were actually listening to. It almost felt like they had got it in for Scott.

I bought the MOJO magazine from a service station whilst I was on the way to a stag weekend in Torquay, Devon. I was heartbroken to be honest and actually cried in my hotel room. Scott really didn't deserve this. I genuinely couldn't fathom it. What did he have to do to get their praise? This was a genuine talent (a musical genius in my opinion) putting heart and soul into his music.

The 'Fractured' single didn't fare much better either. Zane Lowe played the track once and that was it. As for Jo Whiley, well she was nowhere to be seen.

The rest of 2009 was pretty much spent on the road, with UK tours and festivals. Scott made another appearance at Glastonbury, this time playing the acoustic stage. Ex- Kinks frontman Ray Davies was the headline act and being a Kinks fan, I was determined to have a chat and get a photograph. However, on approaching Ray, he appeared to be quite cold. I asked for a photo, but he said "I have to go and get something from my dressing room, can we do it later?" When he re-appeared back stage, Scott's girlfriend Sally said, "Quick go and grab him." But for me the moment had gone. To Sally's credit, she insisted that I ask again. So I did and he obliged. He still seemed quite miserable though. But then he turned to me and asked, "So what do you do?" I said, "I manage a singer/songwriter called Scott Matthews who is performing before you." "Scott Matthews?" he replied. "How is he doing? I love his music." And Ray's mood seemed to change instantly.

Talking of musical icons, there was another amazing meeting in 2009. Scott and I were in London for a couple of meetings, when we got a call from Scott's lawyer Robert Horsfall, "Can you come into the office today? I want you to meet someone." So we popped in and were served coffee whilst we awaited the arrival of the mystery guest. About thirty minutes later Robert's phone beeped and he excitedly got up, announcing, "I will be back in a few minutes." He left the room and ten minutes later, burst through the door with the announcement, "I'd like you to meet Yusuf Islam." We couldn't quite believe it, of course Yusuf was formerly known as Cat Stevens, the brilliant singer-songwriter, responsible for classic songs, such as, 'Father and Son', 'Wild World' and 'Moonshadow'.

Yusuf joined us for coffee and we played him some of Scott's new material and then we were treated to Yusuf's new songs.

Looking back it was slightly surreal. Moments like that certainly have more impact when they are totally unexpected.

As Scott and I left the building, we looked at each other and I said, "Did that just really happen?" We are both big Cat Stevens fans. It was an absolute treat. Thanks Robert.

I have a vivid memory of our last ever meeting at the Island offices. It was quite painful. There were a lot of new staff at the label and so the president, Ted Cockle, thought it would be good if everyone introduced themselves. When it finally got to Louis Bloom, he just said, "Louis Bloom A&R, but unfortunately not for this artist." What he meant by this, was that in his opinion, he felt like he was having very little input in Scott's development. He made it sound like he was trying to do his job, but was intimating that it was Scott, Marco, me, or all three of us that were not allowing him to do so. This really wasn't the case. As with any relationship there are things you agree on, and things you disagree on. I always saw the relationship as a two way street. We are all human and we make mistakes, believe me, Island didn't always get it right.

During the meeting, we talked about various aspects concerning Scott's career and when Ted ended the meeting, he said, "We don't really feel we can entice Scott with anything. There is no carrot we can dangle to get him to do things. I just feel like the label wants it more than he does."

Ted was perhaps dwelling on some of the things Scott had turned down, such as a possible collaboration with the band Faithless and the offer to perform on the Sharon Osbourne Television Show (this wasn't much of a show, but it did get viewing figures of around two million during its first few weeks on air).

By the way, Scott wasn't present in this meeting. Scott had no real interest in the business side of music. I don't think that's unusual and I believe that musicians should do what they do best and create. Scott would often ask if he was required for a specific meeting, and if not, he would happily grab a coffee, or go and shop for guitars.

Just as the meeting was grinding to a halt, Marco, completely out of the blue, turned to Ted and asked, "Can I have that chair?"

In two corners of the room were director style folding chairs, with the Island Records logo on the back rest.

I looked at Marco in total bemusement. What a strange question to ask. Ted looked puzzled and then replied, "Yes, I suppose so."

One by one all the staff left the office, leaving just Marco and me looking at each other. "That's that then," I said.

"Yep, it looks like it."

We both knew deep down that we wouldn't be seeing the Island office again.

They hadn't even offered to escort us out of the building. They just left us sitting there. Marco stood up and folded his newly acquired chair. I looked at the other one and turned to Marco and said, "If you are having a chair, I'm having a fucking chair."

"You can't just take it without asking."

"I can and I am."

I picked it up and we both left the building. We got a few strange looks as we walked along Kensington High Street and when we got to Euston train station, someone asked us, "What you doing with those chairs?" I said, "I just stole it from Island Records." He looked surprised and said, "Cool."

## The Nick Drake, John Martyn tributes and One Shot Not

Scott's deal with Island Records was over. He would be seeing in 2010 right back where he first started, with San Remo Records. Contractually, Scott could have moved to another label but decided to stay with Marco and San Remo.

To be honest, considering Scott was no longer with a major label, 2010 turned out to be a very fruitful year. As well as playing Celtic Connections festival, he was asked to perform in a Nick Drake tribute concert that was being organised by American producer Joe Boyd.

Nick Drake (also signed to Island Records) was a 60s folk artist from Tanworth-in-Arden, Warwick-shire, who never really found fame during his lifetime. He suffered with depression and stage fright, so rarely performed live. Nick died in 1974 from what some believe to be an accidental overdose of antidepressants.

Lots of people are now discovering Nick's albums and many musicians are citing Nick as being a big influence on their own music.

Nick only released three albums, but they are all classics.

Joe Boyd produced two of Nick's albums, *Five Leaves Left* (1969) and *Bryter Layter* (1971).

The Nick Drake tribute was called, 'Way to Blue: The songs of Nick Drake' and featured an eclectic mix of special guests that included Stuart Murdoch, from the band Belle and Sebastian, Eddi Reader, Lisa Hannigan, Vashti Bunyon and Paul Simon's son, Harper Simon. The show toured to The Royal Concert Hall, Glasgow; Brighton Dome,

Barbican Centre, London and Warwick Arts Centre.

It even went to Australia in 2011, which included a show at the prestigious Sydney Opera House.

There is no live footage available of Nick Drake performing, which is a real shame and just one of the reasons why the tribute concert was so well received. It was such a joy hearing Nick's songs played live. Scott performed the songs 'Day is Done' and 'Place To Be'.

It was great that 2010 had started on such a positive note, because if I am honest, I was quite worried about the prospect of moving forward without a major label. I mean the whole relationship hadn't been that successful, but having a major label behind you does carry a certain amount of gravitas.

Scott's contract with San Remo was a four album deal. So in effect there were two albums left to record before Scott's contract would be fulfilled.

We started to plan the recording of the third album and Scott was keen to go full circle and return to work with Jon Cotton, who had recorded Scott's debut album *Passing Stranger*.

The recording was due to start in March 2010, but before that we had to make a trip to Paris for France's equivalent of *Later With Jools Holland*. It was a show called *One Shot Not* and was hosted by drummer extraordinaire Manu Katche. Manu had drummed on Peter Gabriel's massive breakthrough album of 1986 entitled, *So*.

Just like Jools Holland, Manu likes to accompany some of the bands appearing on the show and played drums on the 'Passing Stranger' song. That was really something. I'd have happily taken Manu on tour with us, because he's an amazing drummer.

Only the two of us made the journey to Paris. It was a good trip and gave us plenty of time to talk about the future. In many ways, Scott was more positive now than he had ever been whilst tied to Island Records. I was remaining positive too. It wasn't like Scott hadn't had any publicity, far from it, he'd had plenty. We just had to try and build on that now, by finding new, passionate team members, who believed in Scott's music as much as Marco and I did.

Oh and we would also have to find another booking agent too, because I had fallen out with Mick Griffiths. This was a sad moment. Mick had been there from quite early on and I respected him a lot.

Our falling out was started by a passing comment I had made over the phone. I had been asking Mick if he could source more folk type festivals, which he said he would, but I never really heard back from him. I think it had reached a point where we felt that Scott needed to be playing a lot more festivals. Considering how many festivals were out there, during 2009, Scott only played a handful.

Mick had said that he didn't really feel Scott was a big festival artist and that we should be putting our efforts elsewhere. The thing is, the festivals are a valuable source of income, and it was part of my job to make sure Scott was earning as much as possible.

I called Mick on the phone and was calmly and politely asking if he'd found any more festivals for us. He seemed to be trying to skirt around the subject so I said, "Look Mick, just tell me if you can't be arsed?" Turns out it was the worst thing I could have said and he put the phone down on me. I wasn't nasty and yes, perhaps it wasn't really the right way to phrase the statement.

I couldn't get hold of Mick for two weeks. His assistant told me he was off ill. When I finally got hold of Mick, he said, "I nearly told you to fuck off that day. Oh and you lost Scott money through doing Cropredy 2009, when I told you not to."

Ah yes, Cropredy, now the issue surrounding this particular festival, was that Mick wasn't happy because one of the organisers and members of the band Fairport Convention, Dave Pegg, had contacted Scott directly. I didn't see this as a problem at all. Why would I? But then I think Mick was thinking that Dave should be going through Scott's agent. This seemed petty to me.

Dave was asking Scott to do the festival quite late in the day, so most of the festival acts had long since been booked. However, Mick was trying hard to secure more money and a slot higher up the bill, but without much success. Dave was losing patience and so I eventually overruled Mick's suggestion that Scott should play the festival the following year instead.

Mick decided that he didn't want to contract the show, so I did it myself. In fact, he didn't want anything to do with it. The thing is, if Scott hadn't have played it in 2009 then he simply wouldn't have been asked the following year, of that I am certain. We'd already made it clear that Scott was available and therefore the festival organisers would know that we had literally turned it down, because we wanted more money and someone else's slot higher up the bill.

I had a meeting with Scott and Marco to discuss the idea that we should try and find a new booking agent. They both agreed that at this point, it was

228

the right thing to do. So I sent Mick an email, saying that we were going to find a new agent. There is no contract with booking agents, so you are not tied to them.

In March Scott started recording his third album, which was to be titled *What the Night Delivers.* It was highly unlikely that the new album would come out that same year, so we decided to release a live album entitled, *Scott Matthews - Live in London.*

Back in 2009, Scott had played an acoustic show at Shepherd's Bush Empire and it just so happened, that Scott's sound engineer at the time, Jerry Melcher, had recorded the entire concert. So Jerry set about mixing it and San Remo released it. It was a lovely interim record.

The recording sessions for *What the Night Delivers* had gone really well and after the first listen, it had become my favourite Scott Matthews album. However, the budget had totally run away with itself and it ended up costing a hell of a lot more than we had all hoped. The final figure totalled £39,000. Recoupment wouldn't be easy.

Marco and I discussed the possibility of licensing the album to another label and we both agreed that it wouldn't hurt to at least contact other labels, to see if there was any interest.

This turned out to be quite a stressful time. Scott needed a new publisher, booking agent and I also had to tout Scott's new album around all the record labels. What I didn't expect was to be faced with a wall of indifference.

On the publisher front, I contacted Imagem, Peer Music, Bug Music, Stage Three Music, Sony/ATV, Warner Chappell, EMI and Mute Song.

To be fair, EMI did make an offer, but it wasn't a good one. There was also an offer of an administration deal from Mute Song, but after running it past Scott's lawyer, he advised against it. I wish I had ignored his advice to be honest.

I am not saying that Mute Song would have been a perfect fit, but they did have a much smaller roster than the likes of Universal and they would have been able to dedicate more time to Scott.

On the record label front, amongst others, I contacted Domino Records, Wichita Recordings, Bella Union, Peace Frog, Beggars Banquet and Cooking Vinyl.

The only interest we had was from Peace Frog, but when we travelled to London to meet them, it looked more like a label that was winding down. They seemed like really nice genuine guys, but we just weren't certain that a Peace Frog release would do any better than a San Remo release.

Then finally there were the booking agents. X-Ray Touring, The Agency Group, Primary, ITB, Coda and Free Trade Agency. A couple of agents asked for a copy of Scott's new album, but nothing came of it. I couldn't really understand it. Live shows were a cast iron guarantee of making money. Yes, Scott's audience had dwindled. For example, the Shepherd's Bush show in 2007 was a sell out with 2000 people and his 2010 average for London was around 500. But there were still high profile gigs coming in, the 2010 Celtic Connections show is a good example. There was a healthy fee of £4000. 10% to the agent is £400, couple these kinds of fees with all the other yearly touring money and it's not to be sniffed at, and yet here I was, fighting to get a new agent on board and with no one really showing any interest.

Eventually, my good friend Markus Sargeant came to the rescue and put me in touch with Pete Sangha, a booking agent who worked for Neil O'Brien Entertainment. Pete offered his services, along with DHP Family, who are a Nottingham based promoter and I was able to breathe a sigh of relief.

Just like the *Passing Stranger* and *Elsewhere* albums, *What the Night Delivers* would also feature a special guest, in the shape of Danny Thompson, who was the UK's greatest go-to double bass player.

In fact, Danny has played double bass on some of my favourite albums of all time. He played on David Sylvian's *Brilliant Trees* and *Secrets of the Beehive*; Talk Talk's *Colour of Spring* and *Spirit of Eden*; and Nick Drake's *Bryter Layter*. This is to name but a few. The list of his collaborations is huge.

Danny was also a long-time collaborator and friend of the late, great John Martyn and in 2010 was curator of a show called, 'Grace and Danger, the Songs of John Martyn'. Just like the Nick Drake tribute, 'Grace and Danger' would feature an array of guests, including Beverly Martyn, Ian McNabb, Beth Orton, Eddi Reader and of course Scott.

The show took place at Birmingham Town Hall and really was a night to remember. John Martyn had been such an amazing songwriter, one of his highlights for me being his 1973 album *Solid Air*.

My big regret about the 'Grace and Danger' show was not taking the time to ask Eddi Reader about Stuart Adamson. Eddi had sung backing vocals on Big Country's song, 'Fragile Thing'. The song was taken from their 1999 album *Driving to Damascus,* and is often considered one of their finest songs. It is, however, quite a sad song. It tells a story of lost love and regret. Whenever I listen to it, I can't help but think of it as clear reflection of Stuart's state of mind and how those dark thoughts must have got so much worse, considering that two years later he would no longer be with us.

## The Sea-change

San Remo released *What the Night Delivers* in September of 2011, and both press and online reviews were really good, with the likes of Uncut, The Express and The Daily Mirror all giving the album four star reviews.

Some of Scott's biggest fans within radio loved the album too, Lauren Laverne from 6 Music and Dermot O'Leary from Radio 2 both raved about the album.

The relationship with our new agent got off to a flying start too and we ended up doing 31 UK shows to promote *What the Night Delivers*. It was the longest single run of shows Scott had ever done.

I have to take my hat off to the musicians involved on that tour, because they put their heart and soul into it and for very little money.

I actually tour managed the shows, and got fantastic deals on hotels through early pre-booking. We also got hold of a free trailer, thanks to Scott's guitar tech Jamie Davey. Jamie's brother-in-law, Ian, kindly let us use it for the duration of the tour. All these savings meant that Scott could still earn money from the shows.

We had a new musician on board for this tour, Greg Stoddard. He was a multi-instrumentalist and brought a new dimension to the live shows, some of his electric guitar parts were inspired. He looked great too, very cool and retro, he would often wear a plain fitted shirt and his look reminded me of a young Bernard Sumner during the Joy Division years circa '79. Greg is a quiet chap and would often only speak if there was something really worth saying.

The overall vibe surrounding the *What the Night Delivers* album and tour was great, however, sales were fairly slow and it was quite difficult to see how they would pick up over the coming months.

As we entered 2012, I started having my first pangs of despondency. I called a fellow manager, Paul McDonald for advice. Paul manages the singer/songwriter James Morrison. I had met Paul a few times in the past. He had even asked me if I thought there might be the possibility of James and Scott performing together in the future.

Paul thought that Scott just really needed to deliver a big single now. Something extremely radio friendly. It's difficult though, I mean we all knew the importance of radio, but Scott just isn't the write to order kind of artist.

There was also another significant fact about 2012. It was the first year my business had made a loss. I hadn't been stupid with money, so it didn't feel like the end of the world, but it was still vital for me to try and find a way to turn the business around, and I knew it wouldn't be easy.

All in all 2012 was a fairly quiet year. Of course, Scott was still receiving his regular royalty payments from PRS, MCPS and PPL, but as far as live shows were concerned, there was very little coming in. Agents and promoters are never keen on sending an artist back out on the road immediately after completing a tour. I understand this, but felt there was still plenty of unexplored territory to be mined.

Another problem for us was that we weren't making much leeway abroad. In an ideal world, Scott would have been following his UK dates with a European tour, but the level of fees being offered were often too low to make it work. In fact, Scott only did one date abroad during the whole of

2012, which was a small show in Barcelona.

Scott's fourth album would be recorded in his home studio and titled *Home Part 1*. It was a great collection of songs, but not as stripped back as I expected. Initial discussions were hinting towards a more acoustic, guitar/vocal album. But it didn't turn out that way.

The actual release was dogged with logistical issues.

The first development to delay the release of the album was an email to Scott from Radiohead's guitarist Ed O'Brien, offering to instigate a meeting between Scott and Radiohead's management, ATC.

Ed O'Brien didn't really know anything about Scott's current management set up, he just saw Scott as an amazing artist that should be more successful than he actually was. Indeed, join the club Ed!

Ed told Scott that he had been listening to the *Passing Stranger* album everyday whilst on the way to the studio, during the recording of their *In Rainbows* album. I think Ed had even told Scott that it influenced some of his own guitar parts.

Any potential involvement with ATC was a big deal and a huge opportunity for Scott. I can't really speak for Marco, but personally, I was running on empty. If Radiohead's management were willing to take Scott on, I certainly wasn't going to stand in his way.

We also had interest from Nashville based label Thirty Tigers, who were essentially interested in 'project managing' the new album. So all in all, there were a lot of things to consider.

The ATC issue seemed to drag on forever. Scott went to numerous meetings, but nothing ever seemed to get resolved. The clock was constantly ticking, and we had the album release on hold until we knew exactly how all this ATC stuff was going to pan out.

I sat down with Scott and said, "Look, we are talking about Radiohead's management here. It would be nice to be able to compete with that, but I can't."

I was out of ideas and my naive notion of being able to 'take on the world' had long since left me. My confidence had taken a serious bashing and was at an all-time low.

Marco and I were adamant that Scott would get a management offer from ATC, but said offer never came. In the end I said to Scott, "We need to really start moving forward with the new album. Do you want me to contact ATC and ask them what their intentions are?"

Scott agreed and I sent an email to Brian Message and Neil Simpson at ATC.

The email was basically an overview of Scott's career thus far, and how we had found it difficult over the last couple of years to re-establish Scott's position in the industry.

I also pointed out that we were happy to talk, if ATC were genuinely interested in managing Scott, because first and foremost, I wanted what's best for him. At this point in time, I had zero concern for my own future.

Neil responded with an email stating that, 'At this moment there isn't a management conversation to be had with us.' The email went on to say that they felt Scott had backed himself into a creative place, that was both narrow and insular.

During meetings with Scott, they had mentioned the idea of collaborations, which was never really Scott's bag. He just wasn't into that at all. Thus, I don't think ATC could see how they could move things along, if they didn't share the same view of how things should develop in the future.

So that was an end to that, it was just a shame that it had taken so long to get the answer.

Months had passed and now we just needed to get a release date for *Home Part 1*. Caught between a rock and a hard place, we decided to do a deal with Thirty Tigers. Scott really wanted to explore them, but Marco and I certainly had reservations. I mean, who were they really? What had they done? The problem was that if the new album was a San Remo release and it failed, then I guess Scott would have been thinking that the Thirty Tigers route would have been the better option.

The *Home Part 1* release date was set for 10<sup>th</sup> November 2014.

The album campaign was pretty disastrous. Sarah Silver was Thirty Tiger's UK representative. She had been working in the industry for over twenty years, but I felt that she still approached work with a major label mentality. For instance, her choice of PR for Scott was MBC, one of the biggest PR companies in the country. They hit San Remo with a nice £6000 bill for their services. Sure MBC talked the talk, but the press or lack of, didn't justify that hefty price tag. We didn't really see anything for the money. I said, "Marco, if they have any integrity, they will halve the bill." But of course, they didn't.

I guess that campaign was the straw that broke the camel's back and I announced that I was quitting, but told Scott that I would continue to manage until a suitable replacement had been found. It wasn't long before Sarah Silver offered her services as the new manager.

I don't think she had really managed before, but her business partner, Maurice Bacon had, in fact, he was still managing the band Kula Shaker. Scott seemed to think that the relationship might work. Sarah had a close relationship with Robert Plant too. Maybe this could prove significant in the long run.

My only reservation was that I still kept having this fear that she would not be able to work outside of the old school industry business model. I didn't think it was enough anymore to just throw boat loads of money at an artist, and think things will then take care of themselves. Yes, you need capital, but you have to be very clever with how you spend it.

Technology has changed the game, and there are so many ways that people consume music nowadays, so more investment in new media is vital. You have to have that internet presence.

My final show with Scott was at Birmingham Town Hall, on Saturday 29th November. It was emotional to say the least. I watched the show from the balcony and cried as it came to a close. It was a fantastic night and the band got a standing ovation.

So, my career as a music manager had come to an end. To say I was sad would be an understatement. For a start, I had absolutely no idea where I was going to go from here.

However, it has always been my belief that you have to know when it's time to turn the page.

I contacted all my business associates, to see if they had any jobs available. But I found this quite embarrassing, because it felt like I was going around with a begging bowl. Scott suggested that I should become a tour manager, but I didn't want to spend the majority of the year on the road. Now into my forties, it just didn't seem right to turn around to Jayne and say, 'Right Jayne, take care, see you in three months' time.'

I had spent so much time on the road throughout the years that I was now looking forward to spending more time at home.

The one thing I promised myself, was that no matter what I ended up doing, I would still try and be creative.

## Filmonics

It had been 10 years since the release of *Put the Needle Down and Fly*, when Marco and I began to discuss the possibility of recording a new Fly album.

We had accumulated an abundance of material over the intervening years, so it seemed like the logical thing to do. But after pooling our material together, Marco and I couldn't agree on which songs to use. Some of Marco's tracks were leaning more towards jazz and mine were, for want of a better word, instrumental electro pop.

Try as we might, we just couldn't find any middle ground, so Marco suggested the idea of there being a Fly album... minus me. Ouch!

That hurt quite a lot. I had been an integral part of the first Fly album and I couldn't really bear the thought of Marco and Gary recording a second album without me. But then, out of the blue, Marco called me and suggested that the two of us could do a side project.

I really warmed to this idea and so Marco and I started working on new material.

Spending time in recording studios can be very expensive, so in order to avoid those costs, we both purchased a digital download of the industry standard recording studio, Logic 9. The idea being that we could record the album ourselves, at home.

I would say that a large majority of the contemporary albums you hear are either recorded using Logic or another popular software studio, called Pro Tools.

Logic is a multi-track studio, which comes with

a wide variety of samples and sounds. Everything from percussion, strings and brass, to synthesizers and drum loops.

The beauty of us both using Logic was that we didn't even need to be in the same room to compose. I could send Marco a song, via email. He could then open the file in his version of Logic and add parts to the song, then email it back.

My music set up consists of a Korg MS 2000, Microkorg, Microkorg XL, Yamaha CS1X and a Yamaha SHS-10, but most of my recording was done using the MS2000 as a MIDI (Musical Instrument Digital Interface) keyboard, this means that I wasn't actually using the synthesizer's built in sounds, but using the keyboard to control sounds that are stored in Logic, via my computer.

As well as the sounds stored in Logic, we used a whole host of plug-in synthesizers. These are usually referred to as softsynths. Basically, synthesizers without the hardware. Nowadays, almost every synthesizer you can buy is available to download as a softsynth. These are a lot cheaper than buying the actual keyboard.

As an example, if you want to buy an actual vintage Prophet V synthesizer, assuming you could find one of course, it will probably set you back about £5000.

The softsynth version is £80.

We came up with dozens of names for the new project, but eventually settled on Marco's suggestion, Filmonics. The word film being important, as the new material would lean heavily towards cinematic music, more so than our previous Krautrock leaning Fly album.

I love the writing process. It's just so easy to lose yourself in it.

I usually start by finding a really interesting sound, and then work on a melody. It could be a chord progression, a lead riff or a drum loop.

Slowly, I start to build the song, finding new chord progressions as I go along. It really is a building blocks type of process.

The great thing about digital recording is that it allows you to edit easily too. Nowadays, unless you are recording analogue (onto tape) you don't really need to re-record parts because you can delete wrong notes and paste the correct ones back in.

People often get the wrong impression of electronic music. Some still think you just push a button and the computer does all the work. This really isn't the case. Yes, you can make singers sound better with auto-tune or whatever, but composing still requires actual humans with musical ideas.

I remember seeing an interview with Orchestral Manoeuvres in the Dark's Andy McCluskey. Their eponymous debut album came out in 1980, and at the time, because they were at the forefront of this newly emerging electronic scene, a lot of the traditionalists would slag them off. I guess people just assumed they couldn't really play, or play well at least.

Andy was quick to point out that all the parts on their debut album were played live. They manually layered all the keyboard parts on top of each other. Of course, on the road it was a slightly different story, because you would need to have a lot of musicians onstage to be able to play all the individual keyboard parts, so they made backing tracks on a reel to reel tape machine, which they quirkily named Winston.

I have a lot of respect for Orchestral Manoeuvres. Their debut album was recorded almost entirely using a budget Korg Micro-Preset synthesizer, bought out of a mail order catalogue. It's pure DIY. There's a punk element in there for sure. Buy a cheap keyboard, learn a few chords, write some songs and then make an album. You didn't have to be a virtuoso.

We decided to call our new album *Future Forest*.

Marco would be responsible for designing the artwork, along with our good friend Bruno Cavellec.

The running order would be as follows:
1. Future Forest
2. Silver Street
3. Beyond the Tide
4. New Moon
5. Tokyo
6. The Pendulum
7. Messages
8. What If
9. The Waltz
10. We'll Never Know

The final mixing took place in my dining room and the mastering was done at Mad Hat studios, near Wolverhampton.

We put the album out on Marco's San Remo label, and launched it with a show at Wolverhampton's, Newhampton Arts Centre, on Friday November 14th 2014.

Newhampton Arts Centre is run by my good friend Chris Brown. A man of many talents, Chris is not only a great sound engineer, but a great musician too. He played lead guitar in the

Wolverhampton band, Mudskipper. Ex-Sunny Daze members Paul Cashmore and Ade Beddow were also in the band. I saw them play live many times in the late 90s, and as far as I was concerned, at that time they were the best unsigned band in Britain. That's certainly how I would have described them anyway, had I have been a writer for one of the big music magazines.

They eventually released their debut album *Eggshells* on the Pomona Sounds label, but I think they split up shortly after.

The launch idea was really just to test the material out live, and hopefully sell a few copies of the album on the night.

I hadn't played keyboards on stage for around 10 years, so I was crapping myself. It was worse for Marco, because he had never played keyboards on stage before. The other factor that made me really nervous was the almost total reliance on technology for our show, and the fear that something might break down mid-set.

Altogether on stage, we had three synthesizers, two electric pianos, two Apple Macs and a portable mixing desk. There was certainly plenty of scope for something to go wrong. The computers were used for both the backing tracks and our actual keyboard sounds. We played as much live, as two pairs of hands would allow.

With support from the marvellous Wolverhampton based band, Field Harmonics, all in all, it was a great night. We got lots of friends and family along, including my good friend Lee Harris, who later, on a trip to Japan, shot a couple of videos for the songs, 'Messages' and 'Tokyo'.

## *That was then, this is now*

I worked in the music industry for ten years and never really thought my business would come to an end, but then you don't when you are in the thick of it. However, I was always realistic about what I could achieve and was never really sure that I had the vision to turn Pulse Music Management into a hugely successful company. My strong drive and work ethic aside, sometimes the stars just don't align.

The music industry has changed a hell of a lot over the course of the last few years. Nowadays, it seems to be more show business, than music business.

The cult of celebrity is huge and most of the major players aren't just reliant on music as their sole source of income. You have the likes of Jesse J appearing as a judge on TV show, The Voice and Rita Ora advertising mobile phones. They all diversify.

I consider myself more of an artist, than a businessman. This may have been another reason why I found it difficult to adapt to the demands of the modern music industry. Business has never really interested me and I have never been motivated by money. I am first and foremost a music fanatic. I was never going to be the next Richard Branson.

Island Record's Ted Cockle once said to me, "So do you want to be the next Peter Grant?" (Led Zeppelin's manager). I am not sure if he was being facetious. But I replied with, "No, I want to be Martin Davies."

Scott always made the albums he wanted to make. I am proud of that fact, and it is my belief that every artist should retain creative control, because creative control often leads to great art.

I don't think there are many artists that relish sitting in a record label office, having a bunch of people telling them what they should be doing with their music and artwork. But of course, once you sign the contract and take their money, the label will want to have their say, they will want something back for their investment. I totally get that, but you have to draw the line somewhere.

We found ourselves in that exact position with the re-release of Scott's *Passing Stranger*, when Island Records were adamant on changing the cover.

Did the new cover make a significant difference to sales? It didn't. For me the whole exercise had been pointless.


I always imagined that Scott would have the same type of career trajectory as PJ Harvey. Also on Island Records, PJ seems to have always done things her way, with complete creative control.

She has been able to slowly build her following over a number of years, and perhaps that's the difference, that's what allows her to have total control. You get established, and then you call the shots.

We all hoped the relationship with Island would be long and fruitful. But if the records aren't selling, how long can a label keep throwing money at it?

Could we have done more? Well, I guess you can always do more.


Filmonics has been put on the back burner for the time being, although Marco and I certainly plan to work together again in the future.

I still have lots of unused music, so decided to use the name Chrome Appliance as a solo moniker. I have recently been composing incidental music for a Youtube travel show series called *Cummings Your Way*. It is part humorous, part surreal and steeped in the mystery of old England.

My friend Lee Harris is the filmmaker and the star of the show is Dan Cummings. The pair of them literally travel the length and breadth of the country and usually base each episode in a single location.

One of the first episodes I saw was Shrewsbury, and from that moment on I was hooked. Partly scripted, but mainly ad-libbed, Dan's delivery to camera never falls short of the mark, and his command of the English language is awe inspiring.

When I questioned him about how it all started, he said:

*"I was born in the Black Country in the late nineteen sixties, son of a Londoner and a Lancastrian, and further back of Scots and Irish Lineage. This engendered two things. Firstly, I have a strangely proprietorial sense of the British Isles. They all feel like they belong to me, and secondly I always feel like a tourist, wherever I am.*

*I grew up feeling protective toward Britain, as the decade of my birth had rendered it obsolete as a holiday destination - and particularly protective toward England, as it seemed to suffer in comparison to its cooler Celtic neighbours - for socio -political reasons too well documented to go into here, and, even more peculiarly protective of the English Midlands, which seemed in the public consciousness to serve as an unhappy and indistinct buffer in the friction of the North/South divide.*

*In 1989 I saw Jonathan Meades showcasing the forgotten talent of Ian Nairn on television. A fuse was lit. I knew immediately that this was what I wanted to do with my life but back then there seemed no way of achieving it. I often talked about hosting a travel show about Britain and even started but never finished a short story about a man with my name who becomes legendary for doing so.*

*One of these conversations took place in a house just off Streatham High Road in 1995 and my friend Julie Palmer suggested that it should be called Cummings Your Way."*

Fast forward to 2010, and after mentioning the idea to Lee Harris (both then teachers at St Edmunds Catholic School, Wolverhampton) Lee suggested that they film the idea. So in October 2010, they filmed a pilot in Claverley and Bridgnorth, Shropshire.

As of April 2017, they have shot 31 episodes, nearly all of which contain my compositions.

If only I could follow in the footsteps of Clint Mansell. Clint was lead singer in the Stourbridge 80s/90s band Pop Will Eat Itself. After the group disbanded Clint met film director Darren Aronofsky, who asked him to score the music for his film, *Requiem for a Dream*. That was back in 1996 and now Clint is a well-established film composer, with a string of movie scores under his belt, including *Moon*, *The Wrestler*, *Black Swan* and *Noah*.

*Cummings Your Way* is what one might call guerrilla filmmaking, but it could easily be on terrestrial television, yes it's that good. I actually appear in an a few episodes too.

With a budget behind it, the sky would be the limit. Who knows, after fully exploring the UK, it could go global. I can just picture it, "And now on BBC 2, the second episode of *Cummings Your Way* sees Dan exploring the sights and sounds of Japan." Hey, you got to dream big right? So here's keeping our fingers firmly crossed.

I really did fear reaching the end of this book. I don't know why, it just seemed daunting. It felt like I was drawing a line under the whole experience with Scott, I dunno, like this really meant it was time to move on, which I guess, deep down, I know it is.

I will never forget though, I will never be allowed to, because there will always be reminders. Little coincidences, freakish things that happen to me, sometimes I feel they happen just to rub my nose in it, like when my wife and I were in San Francisco in 2015, trying to locate a coffee shop, after being given not-so-great directions by a rapper who was trying to peddle his CD on the high street.

After we tipped him, he gave us a tip in return; "Don't go to Starbucks for coffee man, if you really want a great drink, you should visit the Blue Bottle."

We eventually located the coffee shop, which was very busy indeed, that's always a good sign. I told Jayne to take a seat and joined the queue. I remember there was a song playing, but I wasn't really paying much attention. The music slowly faded and then I heard the intro to Scott's song, 'Eyes Wider than Before'. I couldn't quite believe it. My mind was saying, 'No, please, not this song, not today.'

Don't get me wrong, it was amazing that this

particular track was playing in a San Francisco coffee shop, but I knew deep down that it would ruin my day. Once that poisoned dart enters the brain, that's it, it just festers there. I spent the rest of the day asking myself, 'What if.' A futile question of course, 'What if we had conquered America?' It was a classic happy/sad moment.

Yes indeed, I will always have to remain on guard, because these little moments will probably continue to happen for the rest of my life.

Now I know I am being quite dramatic here, but come on, I did go to drama school. Please allow me this one moment.

Fast forward to 30<sup>th</sup> April 2017, the day before my 47<sup>th</sup> birthday and here I am in Los Alcazeres, Spain at exactly 10:15am, lying by my sister-in-law's pool. No lifeguard in sight, no one to rescue me from my own thoughts. You have to be so careful not to drown yourself in them. But what thoughts you might ask?

Ah well, it is another one of those freakish moments.

I am lying next to Jayne. The sun's rays are starting to break through the clouds and I slowly begin to drift off into a beautiful and peaceful sleep. I could only have been asleep for a few minutes, when I find myself in the Blue Bottle coffee shop in San Francisco. 'Eyes Wider than Before' is playing and I am sitting on a stool gazing out of the window. The dream lasted seconds, before a noise woke me from my sleep.

As I slowly came round, I could still hear Scott's music. I raised my head and used my hand to shield the sun from my eyes, and I could just make out the silhouette of Jayne's brother-in-law, Craig, standing in the doorway.

"Check this out Mart, Scott's CD is still in my stereo. I love this album. How on earth this didn't sell millions, I will never know."

"Yes, it's one of life's mysteries," I replied.

The 'What ifs' return to me and I rant about the injustices of the music industry, before Jayne stops me and says, "You've got to stop torturing yourself. You keep going round in circles. It's futile."

She's right of course. And then it hit me like a steam train; the whole journey had actually started with Jayne's sister and brother-in-law, on that night we saw Scott supporting The Smiths cover band.

If they hadn't twisted my arm to go to that gig, mine and Scott's paths would probably never have crossed. In this moment, right here, right now, it feels like I have gone full circle.

"Jayne, I think I am finally ready to move on."

"You'll find something else, you always do. And always remember this, it's better to have loved and lost, than to have never loved at all. Ain't that right Craig?"

"It is indeed. Shall I turn the music off now?"

"No, leave it on. In fact, turn it up. Turn it all the way up to 11!"

## Music that accompanied me on this cathartic journey:

Go-Kart Mozart – *On the Hot Dot Streets*
Ra Ra Riot – *The Orchard*
Big Country – *Steeltown*
Talk Talk – *Spirit of Eden*
Mystery Jets – *Radlands*
Sonic Youth – *Rather Ripped*
Murray A Lightburn –*Mass:Light*
Genesis – *A Trick of the Tale*
Phoenix –*Bankrupt*
Dirty Three – *Toward the Low Sun*
New York Dolls – *New York Dolls*
65DaysofStatic – *Wild Light*
Father John Misty – *Pure Comedy*
PJ Harvey – *The Hope Six Demolition Project*
Amon Duul 2 – *Yeti*
British Sea Power -*Let the Dancers Inherit the Party*
Slowdive – *Slowdive*
Manic Street Preachers – *Journal for Plague Lovers*
Nick Cave - *Skeleton Tree*
The Chameleons – *Script of the Bridge*
Scott Matthews – *Home Part 2*

### Where are they now?

**Alan Davies & Sandra Davies:** Retired and still living in my childhood home in Moxley.

**Jayne Davies:** Currently a store manager at Tesco. We are still together after nearly thirty years, in fact, the only time we argue is when I play David Sylvian's album *Manofon* in the house.

One of her friends from work once bought her a Marmite tin as a Secret Santa. I asked why on earth she had been given such a gift, as I had never seen her eat Marmite. I said, "That's a revelation!"

Jayne's reply was, "Really, a revelation! Finding out you had been taking cocaine, now that's a fucking revelation!"

**Ian Davies:** Working as a roofing estimator and living with his girlfriend Avril in Shepherd's Bush, London. Ian has a daughter named Caitlin. Avril has three children, Janet, Adam and Daniel.
Avril once lived in Jamaica and saw Bob Marley live at Reggae Sunsplash in 1979!

**Dawn & Craig Hadley:** Living in Los Alcazares, Spain. Craig used to be a mechanic for world Speedway champion Greg Hancock.

**Andrew Southall-Owen:** Married to Sue and living in Wolverhampton. They have two awesome children, Lilly and Teddy.

**Paul Southall-Owen:** Married to Marie and living in Canada. They also have two awesome children, Sophie and Tommy.

**Harry Southall-Owen:** Living in Spain with Val. Harry still loves to sing.

**Craig 'Johno' Johnson:** Born to play bass guitar. Johno no longer supplies drugs to his friends. He is living in Wednesbury with his wife George and two beautiful children, Dylan and Elliott. Johno's biggest regret is walking past Jeff Buckley onstage at Glastonbury 1995 to go and watch Supergrass. Jayne and I are Dylan's godparents.

**Rob 'Jacko' Phillips:** As far as I know, he still lives in Wolverhampton, but hasn't been seen since he tried to strangle Lewi during the Christmas of 2001. I lost a friend that day. I was working at the theatre when this occurred. I regret not being there to split the two of them up. Johno and I chose sides. It was wrong. Jacko, I am truly sorry.

**Paul 'Lewi' Lewis:** Lives in Bridgnorth with his girlfriend Helen. We no longer see each other. I certainly feel there is a large amount of guilt over the fight with Jacko. Lewi once said to me, "I would never hit Jacko, but I had to because I couldn't breathe."

**Adrian Matthews:** Lives in Cannock. Every fortnight we go on a record hunt/drinking session. He is a fan of real ale. I am not.

**Mick Biddulph:** Mick lives in Wolverhampton. He works as an electrician and still has a love of scooters. I have so many happy memories with this great man.

**Wayne Stokes**: Lives in Kingswinford with his wife Lisa and two children, Alicia and Chiara. Wayne runs a very successful martial arts school called, The School of Black Belts.

**Alison Wollohan:** Jayne's best friend lives in Claverley with her husband Sean and their two children Shay and Sienna.

**Andy Muckley:** We recently met after years of not seeing each other. Andy no longer plays the drums. He now flies model aircraft. I recently went along as a spectator and it was brilliant. He lives in Bradley and is married to Diane.

**Keith & Ann Berridge:** Keith runs two companies; Concept International Group and the super cool fashion label, David Watts Clothing. Ann also works for the company. They live in Wolverhampton and have three children, Jake, Alex and Lucy. Jayne and I are Jake and Alex's godparents.

**Al Barrow:** Still plays bass with Magnum. He's also a great photographer. He now lives in Chattanooga with his wife Rachael.

**Markus Sargeant:** A true gentleman in every sense of the word. Markus is the music promoter for Glee Club. We regularly meet to talk about life and music over a coffee and a slice of Wensleydale fruit cake.

**Chris Brown:** Lives in Wales with Anna and continues to run the best music venue in Wolverhampton, Newhampton Arts Centre. Check out his new band, Ceri Ridge Trading Company.

My only gripe is that I don't see enough of him! I promise to make more of an effort.

**Paul Cashmore:** Lives near Chris Brown in Wales, with Shayna and their two children Lily and Peter. We can go for over a year without speaking then pick up like we had only spoken two days ago. Currently plays bass in Ceri Ridge Trading Company.

**Paul Martin**: Sadly passed away in November 2006. RIP buddy x

**Ade Beddow:** One of the nicest people you could ever wish to meet. Last I heard he was working as a paramedic. I need to track him down.

**Steve Moxon:** Was spotted a few years ago by my sister-in-law, Dawn. He was busking in Wolverhampton city centre, singing the Sunny Daze classic, 'Follow me'. Current whereabouts unknown.

**Kirstie Phillips:** Lives in Wolverhampton with her husband Lee and daughter Phoebe. We recently talked about the idea of writing some songs together.

**Lee Harris:** Lives in Wolverhampton with Deb and her son Daniel. Lee is Head of Year and teaches English and Film Studies at St. Edmund's Catholic School. He's still a huge music fan and one day we plan to duet a Nick Cave song at Karaoke. Trouble is, we are not sure we could top our rendition of A-ha's 'Take on Me'. We knocked that one out of the ball park.

**Dave Murphy:** Living in Manchester and currently Head of Creative for Baker Media Group at Rock FM. He is married to the lovely Liz. I was best man at his wedding, and yes, I mentioned *The Sword of Tipu Sultan* story in my speech. They have two amazing children, Tom and Charlotte. Dave also has two beautiful children from a previous marriage, named Jack and Becky.

**Sue Hay:** Like a second mother. Now retired, but always busy. She is an amazing theatre director and works regularly with Pattingham Players and Studio 61 in Wolverhampton.

**Owen Lewis:** My brother from another mother. Owen works as a playwright. He wrote *The Astounding Works of Simon Trout*, published by Off The Wall Plays.

**Rich Goodall:** We literally speak on a daily basis. Rich runs his own computer shop called IT Again. He is an amazing bass player and is currently playing bass with bands, Into the Hurricane and Delta Rhythm.

**Ian Davies (DJ):** Still the best DJ in Wolverhampton. Currently DJs a night called Stay Loose. I haven't seen him for a while, but spoke to him on the phone quite recently and we greeted each other in the usual way, "Yo Davo!"

**Claire Allen:** Living in Kingswinford with her husband Barry and three children, Daniel, Caitlin and Emily. Claire is a charity worker for a self advocacy charity.

**Angie Athay-Hunt:** Currently working as a

freelance theatre practitioner. She lives in Bristol with Taff and their three children, Edie, Leo and Ned.

**Marco Thomas:** Lives in Essington with his wife Simone and their two children George and Lydia. Marco continues to look after the San Remo Records back catalogue.

**Gary Ainge:** Still living in London with Lisa and their two children, Mia and Lillian.
He's my favourite drummer. I never did get over that occasion though, where I had to wait downstairs in the Barfly, as The Strokes played their first ever London show upstairs. Gaz tried to get me in, but it was always going to be a tall order.

**Jon Cotton:** Runs a production company called Poseidon Music, which produces feature film soundtracks and music used by NASA, SpaceX and BBC news.

**Bruno Cavellec:** Lives on the Isle of Man with his wife Jill. Bruno works full-time as an artist. Look him up, he's amazing.

**Steve Kray and Aisling O'Reilly:** Continue to run their successful Katch 22 production company. They now have a son called James.

**Pete Machen:** Still acting and writing. Pete wrote and starred in the 2017 film, *Just Charlie*. His daughter Elinor Machen-Fortune also stars in the film. He lives in Manchester.

**Rebekah Fortune:** Director and filmmaker. She

directed the 2017 film *Just Charlie*. Her daughter is Elinor Machen-Fortune.

**Gabby Meadows:** Has a gorgeous boy named Theo. Currently living in Norwich. We are going to meet up soon! I promise.

**Darren Daly:** Currently doing his PhD. He still supports Arsenal and lives in Derby with his wife Carol.

**Scott Matthews:** Lives in Wolverhampton. He got married to his long term girlfriend, Sally, in 2016. I was an usher and gave a reading. He has recently released his brilliant new album, *Home Part 2* on his own independent label, Shedio Records.

**Sam Martin:** The legend that is. Sam is such a great guy to be around. He's played in more bands than any other person I know. Sam is currently living in Stoke. He is a drum teacher and continues to work with Scott Matthews.

**Danny Keane:** The man born to play the cello. I can't keep up with him to be honest. He constantly seems to be touring the world.

**James (Jamie) Davey:** Continues to work as Scott Matthews' guitar tech. He also has his own company called J Davey guitars. Jamie both repairs and makes guitars. He lives in Wolverhampton with his wife Elaine. They have two children, Ben and Jay.

**Greg Stoddard:** One of the coolest musicians on earth. Greg lives in Bristol and is currently working as a course leader at Bristol Institute of Modern Music.

**Louis Bloom:** Last I heard he was head of A&R at Island Records.

**Nick Gatfield:** The former President of Island Records became chairman and CEO of Sony Music UK in 2011. In 2015, he founded Twin Music Inc.

**Mick Griffiths:** Still runs his own booking agency called Art & Industry, representing the likes of Mogwai, Julian Cope, Ocean Colour Scene and Joanna Newsom.

**Robert Horsfall:** Formerly of Lee and Thompson, the highly experienced music lawyer founded Sound Advice in 2008. His current client list includes Yusuf Islam, Ali Campbell and Pendulum.

**Pete Sangha:** Pete is still working as a booking agent for Neil O'Brien Entertainment.

*************

*Remembering Kathleen Ann Southall-Owen (1943 – 2013) A wonderful wife, mother, grand-mother and mother-in-law.*

I know there are a lot of names on this list, but the majority of these people are still in my life. Which if you think about it is pretty remarkable.
Peace and love to you all.
Martin x

# ACKNOWLEDGMENTS

I would like to thank Lee Harris for his advice, guidance and proof reading skills. Thank you, Marnie Summerfield Smith. You gave me so much of your time with advice and words of encouragement, when I was losing the will to finish this book.

Thanks to Jason Sheldon for helping out with photo copyrights.
Very special thanks go to Marco Thomas and Scott Matthews (what a ride guys!)
Without these two people, this book would never have been written.

Cover by the magnificent Bruno Cavellec.

Back cover blurb by Lee Harris.

Book formatted by Rebecca Emin.

Printed in Great Britain
by Amazon